SELLING
ART 101

ArtNetwork

SELLING ART 101, THE ART OF CREATIVE SELLING

Copyright ©2004 by Robert Regis Dvořák

Cover and layout by Laura Ottina Davis

Sketches throughout book by Robert Regis Dvořák

Published by ArtNetwork, PO Box 1360, Nevada City, CA 95959-1360
800. 383.0677 530.470.0862 530.470.0256 Fax
www.artmarketing.com <info@artmarketing.com>

ArtNetwork was created in 1986 with the idea of teaching fine artists how to earn a living from their creations. In addition to publishing art marketing books and newsletters, ArtNetwork also has a myriad of mailing lists—which we use to market our products—available for rent. See the back of this book for details.

The author, Robert Regis Dvořák, may be contacted at PO Box 370371, Montara, CA 94037
650.359.1288 916.391.5051 Fax www.youcreate.com <robert@youcreate.com>

Dvořák, Robert Regis

  Selling art 101 : the art of creative selling / Robert Regis Dvořák. -- 1st ed. --
  Nevada City, CA: ArtNetwork, 2004.

  p. ; cm.
  (101 series)

  Includes index.
  ISBN: 0-940899-86-8

  1. Art--Marketing. 2. Art--Economic aspects. 3. Selling. I. Title.

N8600 .D86 2004
706/.8/8--dc22   0404

Printed and bound in the United States of America

FOREWORD

If you have decided to go into the business of making your living from the sale of your artwork, learning the techniques in this book is a must. Without this information you might make a few sales, but more than likely, you'll miss a lot more!

Learning sales skills does not happen overnight. You must practice and break through some personal roadblocks. You must believe in your work without waivering.

When I took Robert's class through The Learning Exchange in Sacramento, California, I could see by the role-playing exercises we engaged in as students that all of us had a lot to learn and overcome regarding attitude about art sales. I also learned that many of the artists did not have even the simplest of marketing skills, let alone sales skills.

Not only must you read this book, but you must reread and practice, again and again. Try to make the exercises in this book part of your life. As is explained in Chapter 4, you want to reach the fourth skill level—have selling techniques become a natural habit.

Make this book your friend. Fray the edges. Write in it. Mark it up. Put Post-it notes where you need them. After all, it is essentially a workbook.

With the other books in the series, *Art Marketing 101, Art Office, Art Licensing 101* and *Internet 101*, artists can no longer complain about not knowing how to approach their career. All the help a fine artist needs is right in front of you. You simply need to follow through, take your life into your own hands and proceed with an attitude of success. You will be surprised at what awaits you around the corner.

Constance Smith
Author of *Art Marketing 101*

TABLE OF CONTENTS

Chapter 1   Preparing for the Marketplace

Chapter 2   Why People Buy Art

Chapter 3   Client Rapport

Chapter 4   Sales Skills

Chapter 5   Word Power

INTRODUCTION

More than a billion dollars are generated each year with art sales. Every year, many graduates of art schools enter the marketplace eager to make a name for themselves in the art world. Today more people visit art museums than attend baseball games. We see art everywhere—in hotel rooms, lobbies, shopping centers, airports, public centers, private homes and gardens, corporate board rooms, restaurants, hospitals, offices, parking structures and government buildings. Someone bought all this artwork. And someone sold it to them.

More than half a million people are involved in the art world, yet the transfer of a work of art is still a one-to-one business. As in all businesses, there are honest individuals and there are some shady characters with not much integrity. The business of selling art attracts extremely competitive individuals and people seeking fame and fortune. Many artists don't want to have anything to do with this competitive business, this commercial endeavor, and would just as soon stay tucked away in a safe studio working on their inspirations, waiting to be discovered.

Creativity, personal commitment and individual expression are the essence of the artist's soul. Artists must create art even if they have to give up creature comforts. They have no choice. An artist has a passion and a need to create. The making of art requires commitment and energy. So does the selling of art. If you are an artist who wants to sell your work, or if you are a person who wants to sell other people's artwork, maintain the highest integrity. Be professional in your selling endeavors. Use the material in this book to bring something precious—art, and the appreciation of art—to the world around you.

WHAT THIS BOOK IS ABOUT

This book is about the business of selling art, face to face, eyeball to eyeball. For most people, the skill of selling art needs to be learned.

If you study the methods provided in this book, you will find that the approach to selling that I recommend is a gentle one. People love to buy art. People love to own art. Art enriches people's lives. Art can transform consciousness. The artwork displayed in a home will influence the lives of the people who live in that home.

Do not think that I am going to give you a series of techniques that will trick people into buying art. Assume that the people who are interested in the work you are selling would like to own it. I want to assist you in giving people the opportunity to own what they already know they want.

WHOM THIS BOOK IS FOR

Being an artist is exciting. An artist exercises personal creativity and offers it to society. But an artist must also learn the business of being an artist. The great artists who became successful in their lifetime did that. An artist can think of him- or herself like a business. The making of the art is the production department. Then there are the marketing, advertising, public relations, publicity, human resources, sales staff, accounting and bookkeeping department. An individual artist deciding to go into business must see that all these tasks are taken care of in order to be successful. Some successful artists have made lucrative arrangements with art galleries to handle much of this work.

Most artists would prefer to have an art dealer or representative sell their work. It's been my experience, however, that an artist who can sell his or her own work is much more desirable to an art gallery or an art representative. This book is, therefore, written to assist artists of all media—painters, printmakers, graphic artists, sculptors, ceramists, glass workers, jewelry artists, quilt makers, dress makers, craftspeople—as well as an artist's representative—art dealers, art gallery owners and their employees and sales managers, members of co-op galleries, art consultants, art representatives, people engaged in estate sales—anyone who is serious about dramatically increasing art sales. Studying this book will help you gain the necessary confidence to sell your own or others' artwork.

Almost every time I enter an art gallery, I am surprised by the way I am greeted and treated by the gallery staff. Few art galleries take the time or invest the money to properly train their staff. It is rare for me to enter an art gallery and be made to feel so comfortable that I can really enjoy the work and even consider buying a work of art. Gallery owners and staff will indeed benefit from the material in this book.

This book also will be of assistance to those of you who sell at art fairs. In fact, if you are an emerging artist, I recommend you do some street-fair selling to practice these methods.

This book, *Selling Art 101,* is specifically about the process of selling art. I highly recommend ArtNetwork's other books and particularly the companion book to this, *Art Marketing 101,* to help you find your market, solicit a gallery, and become a success at the business of creating and selling art.

WHAT YOU WILL LEARN

If you study *and practice* the material in this book, you will learn:

➤ what to say to a potential buyer,

- ➤ what not to say to a potential buyer,
- ➤ how to talk on the telephone to a potential client,
- ➤ how to prospect for clients,
- ➤ how to take responsibility for the selling process,
- ➤ how to connect a buyer emotionally and intellectually to a work of art,
- ➤ how to test close and then close a sale, and
- ➤ how to ask for referrals.

I hope you will learn that the selling process is fun and satisfying. And there's a bonus here as well: You will learn that the material in this book can be applied to many aspects of your life. Because, indeed, we are selling ourselves every day.

HOW TO USE THIS BOOK

You must practice sales techniques in order to be successful. Don't expect this process to occur overnight. Do the suggested exercises. Use the words and phrases suggested at appropriate times.

Most importantly, you must have the attitude that you *can* sell art. Only with proper skills can you arrive at that attitude. Selling is creative, fun, challenging and satisfying. The more success you have, the more confidence develops.

At the end of each chapter is a suggested list of actions to take. Use these as a guideline to your daily practice of the art of selling art.

HOW THIS BOOK CAME TO BE

When I made the decision to make my living as an artist, I had no idea that I was beginning a long educational program that would result in many disappointments and frustrations, as well as victories and successes. In those beginning years, I used to have an open studio every December for the purpose of selling current work. Before I had a real studio, I would have my open studio in my home. I would move aside the furniture and turn my home into an art gallery. We had nice hardwood floors in the duplex we were living in, and it was not difficult to transform the lower floor into a gallery with my paintings on the walls and tables. I had a guest book, and I sent out invitations to a select list of people. My thinking was that this was a good time to have an open studio because people were looking for special gifts to give their family and friends at Christmastime. I always had moderate success.

After a few years went by, I "graduated" to a commercial studio space. My first open studio at this location was to be a special event. I had a catering service deliver food. I served wine and kept my studio open all weekend. I thought that I had done everything right. I sent out invitations to all of the people on my mailing list. The weather was perfect.

At the end of this open studio, when I took account of all the sales that had been made, I found that my returns were very disappointing. Although I was confident that my new artwork was of the highest quality and had great appeal, I had sold very little. A friend of mine, hearing of my frustration, handed me a tape by the nationally known sales trainer Tom Hopkins. The title of the tape was, *How to Handle Failure and Rejection.* After listening to this tape, I got very excited about the material and asked my friend if he had more tapes by Tom Hopkins. My friend gave me another tape, and then another and another. Eventually I listened to every tape in this album, which was titled, *How to Master the Art of Selling Anything.* I was very naive at that time in my life. I had no knowledge about selling and didn't think it was necessary to have sales training in order to sell. My naiveté turned into excitement as I studied this material as well as other material offered by other sales trainers.

After tailoring the sales techniques I learned to the business of selling art, the sales of my own artwork increased exponentially. I also realized that this material would be helpful to anyone who would like to learn to sell art. I then created a one-day workshop for artists and art dealers, which I called *The Art of Selling Art.* That was the beginning.

Since then, as an art sales consultant, I have presented lectures and many one-day seminars on the subject of selling art. I have also worked with numerous art galleries and individual clients offering art-focused sales training to artists, gallery staffs, and art representatives.

After Constance Smith, the owner of ArtNetwork took my seminar, *The Art of Selling Art,* she asked me if I would be interested in writing this book. I feel that this book together with her own book, *Art Marketing101,* are an invaluable source of information for any person who wants to sell art.

ACKNOWLEDGEMENTS

I would like to acknowledge all of the people who have participated in the many workshops that I have presented for art galleries, universities, colleges and learning centers. Some of their comments are included in this book.

ARTIST'S BIO

Robert Regis Dvořák, FAAR paints in watercolor, oil, and acrylic, with a studio at the Sanchez Art Center in Pacifica, California. His inspirations are the California coast, Hawaii, Yosemite National Park, Europe—particularly Italy and Greece—and the human figure. His watercolors and oils are shown at the Garden Gallery in Half Moon Bay, California, the 20th Street Gallery in Sacramento, The Village Gallery in Maui, and the Nohea Galleries in Honolulu, Hawaii.

Mr. Dvořák also teaches drawing and watercolor classes for University of California Extensions, San Francisco State University's College of Extended Learning, community colleges in California and Hawaii, and the University of Hawaii. He taught architectural design and drawing and watercolor painting at the University of Oregon for seven years and at the University of California at Berkeley for two years.

Mr. Dvořák has written and illustrated the following books: *Drawing Without Fear, The Magic of Drawing, The Pocket Drawing Book, Experiential Drawing*, and *Productivity at the Workstation*. He has illustrated two guidebooks, *Half Moon Bay Exploring on the North Central California Coast* and *Monterey Peninsula Exploring,* by Nancy and Neil Evans. Robert and his work were featured in two articles in *American Artist Magazine*: *"Sketching While Traveling in Greece"* and *"Twenty Minutes to a Beautiful Figure."*

Mr. Dvořák received his Bachelor of Architecture degree from the University of Illinois and his Master of Architecture Degree from the University of California, Berkeley. He was a recipient of the American Academy in Rome Fellowship (two years), two grants from the University of Oregon, and a grant from the California Arts Council to promote art in California schools. He has produced more than 20 short experimental films; many have been featured in film festivals in the US, Europe, and Australia.

Mr. Dvořák has had 22 one-man exhibitions of his work. He is primarily a painter but also works with skill at life drawing and as a printmaker (etchings and woodcuts). His paintings, films, and prints are in many private and museum collections.

Mr. Dvořák has traveled in 54 countries. He has celebrated Carnival in Trinidad; worked as a caricature artist in Japanese night clubs; explored over 10,000 miles of India; bicycled around the Zuider Zee in the Netherlands; investigated the ruins of Angkor Wat in Cambodia; traveled on the Transiberian Railroad; hiked the Great Wall of China; climbed to the top of the Great Pyramid in Egypt; and sailed the Greek Islands.

Mr. Dvořák is often invited to be a keynote speaker and sales trainer, drawing on his many experiences to illustrate his message that every person has the power to see and create his or her life.

Reproductions of a few of his works can be viewed on his web site at www.youcreate.com.

Chapter 1
Preparing for the Marketplace

Making a commitment

Preparing to sell

Prospecting

The three P's

Overcoming roadblocks

The payoffs

If you aren't going to go all the way, why go at all?   Joe Namath

MAKING A COMMITMENT

As an artist, you are probably passionate, very individualistic, have strong personal views, notice things that seem to go unnoticed by others; you dream, you visualize. You are sensitive and idealistic and maybe considered a little crazy by others. You love to create! And, if you are like me, you have trouble balancing your checkbook.

BODY OF WORK

If you are an artist who wants to sell your work, you need to have a body of work—a number of paintings, prints, sculpture pieces, whatever you do, at minimum 12 to 20 pieces—that look like they were done by the same person, are all about the same size, are all in the same medium, are all completed, and have a contextual theme. Don't even attempt to go to an art gallery in search of representation unless you have that. Do not take an assortment of media and subject matters to a gallery, thinking that you will impress the gallery owner by your wide range of talent and skill. The work that you will show must be of the highest caliber—only your very best work. Don't risk showing second-rate work.

Think of the painters and sculptors who are well known—Georgia O'Keeffe, Mark Rothko, Willem De Kooning, Robert Rauschenberg, Helen Frankenthaler, Henry Moore, Andy Warhol, Alberto Giacometti, J. M. W. Turner. Each artist's work has unique subject matter, is consistent in medium, and has a contextual theme.

Art dealers are looking for new work. Do not imitate the successes of others. If a dealer or critic sees a resemblance to another artist, you will not be welcome. You may borrow knowledge and information, but you must do your own work.

Making a commitment in writing reinforces that commitment four-fold.
Constance Smith

When you have a body of work and feel prepared psychologically to sell, be very discriminating. Pick your best, most original and creative works and go for it!

PREPARING TO SELL

I knew a man who saved up enough money so that he could paint in a studio every day for a year to develop a body of work. His work went through many transformations. He had some fine works at the end of this time, but he didn't think he was ready. Since he was out of money, he ended up getting a 9-5 job and never showed the work. Don't wait for perfection. When you think you might be ready, you are ready!

➤ Be sure that you are willing to sell the artworks you create. Ask yourself: Are you willing to have someone else take possession of these works, knowing that you may never see them again? I meet many artists in my *Art of Selling Art* seminars who are just not ready to let their works be sold. If you have done some great work, work that surpasses anything else you have ever done, you may not be ready to see it sold. If you are in that situation, take the best (or your favorite two or three pieces) and keep them for yourself. Then let the others be put up for sale.

➤ When you are creating a new work, always say to yourself, "This work (painting, sculpture, print) is going to be for sale." When you know from the start that you will be letting this one go, you will create with this in mind. As an artist, it is very easy to identify with your creative endeavors. They are like your children in some ways. You feel like they are a part of you. It can be hard to let them go to another home. It is psychologically easier if you know a work's destiny from the start.

➤ Know that you have a gift. Remember that you are offering the world something unique and personal. What you are selling is precious—it has come from your creative spirit. Whether you have been recognized or not, hold on to your personal vision and your self worth. The making of art is something that you must do. Even if no one ever sees your work, you are still creating it. If you want to sell your work, there are many suggestions in this book that will help you do that. As a fellow artist, I know with regard to the

If you have only completed two or three pieces that you really like, you are not ready.

17

*Use your creative talents
in the sale of your work.*

creating that I have no choice. With the selling of the art, however, I do have a choice.

The best way to process this information is to practice it a little at a time. Most importantly, you must have the attitude that you *can* sell art. As an artist, when I began selling my own works, it was scary, even terrifying. But as I became more knowledgeable about the process of selling, I found it to be creative, fun, challenging and satisfying. The more success I had, the more my confidence increased and the process of selling became challenging and enjoyable. With success came a desire to learn more about the process. Begin the process of learning to sell art with an open and creative mind.

COLD CALLS

There are two kinds of cold calls—the incoming call from a potential new client and the outgoing call to someone you've never met.

The incoming cold call is the easier to handle. Someone who is interested in knowing more about the art you are selling calls you. The best way to handle this situation is to set up an appointment so that you can show the art work to them. When you meet, you can apply the selling suggestions from this book.

The outgoing cold call is the more difficult. If you have had some experience making cold calls and feel comfortable doing that, I suggest you work that way. For most of us, however, making a cold call is difficult and often discouraging. I find that there are so many other ways of reaching out to clients that it is not necessary to do this.

WARM CALLS

I try to make what I call "warm calls" to people who I've briefly met, people with whom I've had some previous contact, or people who have been referred to me by other clients. Each situation is different. Here is a list of people who you might want to consider for your warm call prospecting.

➤ Friends of friends

➤ Friends of people who have bought art from you

➤ Parents of the children with whom your children play

➤ Members of the clubs to which you belong: PTA, tennis, golf, book, bridge, gym

➤ Your neighbors

➤ Fellow office workers

➤ Your real estate agents or mortgage brokers

➤ People you meet in the art world

➤ Art gallery owners

➤ Participants in seminars you attend

PROSPECTING

I find that the harder I work, the more luck I seem to have.
Thomas Jefferson

> ➤ Anyone you meet

> ➤ People you sit next to on planes and trains

> ➤ People you meet on cruise ships

> ➤ Artists and people working in the art business

Contacts with any of these people could bring in sales. As you can see, they would not be cold calls, but warm ones.

MORE IDEAS

➤ I have never done this, but I have met artists who have gone door to door in a neighborhood selling their art work. They told me that they were successful in doing this.

➤ Painting on location. People will notice you and stop to inquire. If you are friendly with them, you can build rapport and eventually make a sale. I have sold quite a few paintings to people who have watched me paint on location. I know an oil painter who told me that every time she painted on location and there was a house in the painting, the owner of the house would come over to her and inquire if he could buy the painting.

➤ Have a private reception. Ask a friend or a friend of a friend with a lovely house in an upscale neighborhood to sponsor a reception for you with the purpose of displaying your work on a Saturday or Sunday afternoon. You display your art and the house owner invites her wealthy friends to view your works. You meet these wonderful people, make friends, collect their addresses and phone numbers in your reception book. Even if they don't buy from you that afternoon, they are potential buyers in the future. Each of these people will also be a resource for other referrals. The house owner provides the display space, the food and the beverages. In exchange for this huge favor, you give the owner one of your original paintings. After the reception, you can call all visitors and ask for an appointment. If the home owner is not receptive to this idea, ask for a referral. The key to this idea is to follow up with telephone calls to these individuals. For an artist who is just beginning, this is a wonderful way to launch a career. You will be surprised how people will help, especially if they love the work.

Remember, it is our attitude much more than our aptitude that will determine our success.

WHEN SOMEONE SAYS NO

It often requires a few "No's" before you will receive a "Yes." Don't think that because you hear a no, it means never. You may have to contact a person a number of times before he or she will become interested. As an artist's career grows, people will become more interested. People know that as an artist gets better known, the artwork becomes more expensive. When people see that the artist is determined and her career is moving ahead, they will be more inclined to buy before the art becomes too expensive.

Ignorance is not bliss, it's oblivion.
Philip Wylie

THE THREE P'S

The pictures in your mind will create the reality you find.

A simple way to strategize your success in selling art is to divide your activities into three logical steps.

PICTURE IT

You must picture your greatest success and how it will look. Do whatever you can to see that picture. Close your eyes and imagine. Create a collage of cuttings from magazines that show your success as you want it to be. If you are an artist, you may want to draw or paint the success picture you want to see. To the degree that you are able to picture yourself being the person you want to be, having the experience of success you want to have, and doing what you want to do with your life, that is the degree to which you will find yourself living your picture.

Next, picture your activities on a day-to-day basis. For example, if you have a meeting with a potential buyer, picture yourself having a good rapport with that person. Finally, picture yourself writing up the order.

Do this for every activity you think important and worthwhile. I practice this and I can tell you that it works. You will be amazed when you learn the power of the pictures in your mind. It is one of the most important exercises you can do. It is free and it only takes a few moments.

PLAN IT

The next P is to plan your action. Organize yourself so that you do first things first. Every significant accomplishment has to start with a plan. Call it the blue print for success. Plan your learning, your practice, your prospecting for clients, your selling strategies. If you are an artist, you need to plan what you will be selling and for how much. Look at how much you will need to sell every year to support yourself without working at another job. Plan how much time you will need to devote to that activity. Plan how you will create the work, how many pieces, what size they will be, how much your materials will cost, etc. Write down your plan and then go to the last P.

PROMOTE IT

The third P stands for promote. You will need to promote your mental picture and plan. You may need to get others involved to help you promote this vision. If your vision is generous and noble, you will find it easy to enroll others in your project.

Enthusiasm is the element of success in everything. It is the light that leads and the strength that lifts people on and up in the great struggles of scientific pursuits and of professional labor. It robs endurance of difficulty and makes pleasure of duty.
Bishop Doane

OVERCOMING ROADBLOCKS

To be a success at anything, one must be very well organized.
Charlie Chaplain

EXERCISE

Write down all the reasons why you don't or can't sell art the way you would like to. Don't look ahead at the text. Do this exercise first. See how many reasons you can come up with on your own. You will surprise yourself. There are probably a lot more factors holding you back than you think.

For example: "I'm a procrastinator."

_____

_____

_____

_____

_____

_____

_____

_____

_____

_____

The following list was put together by students in one of my *Art of Selling Art* seminars. It is a pretty good list but far from being all inclusive. You will probably come up with some reasons why you don't sell art the way you would like that are not on this list. You may, however, find some reasons on the following list that should be on your list too. If so, add them now.

➤ I'm a procrastinator.

➤ I'm afraid I will be turned down or rejected.

➤ When it comes to selling, I haven't had any training.

➤ I don't know what to say.

➤ I don't know how to approach a potential client.

➤ I'm not confident in my presentation skills.

➤ I can't talk people into it.

➤ My goals aren't clear enough.

➤ I need some negotiation skills.

➤ I don't know how to close.

➤ I don't follow up.

➤ I don't know how to prospect.

➤ I need some telephone techniques.

➤ I don't know how to take control.

➤ I'm not assertive enough.

➤ I have a poor self-image.

➤ I need more confidence.

➤ I need to organize a sales approach.

➤ I'm in a period of low motivation.

➤ I'm too tired to work at it.

➤ I don't have time.

➤ I haven't made the commitment.

➤ I'm afraid to ask for a fair price.

➤ I am afraid I will fail.

➤ Artists shouldn't be salespeople.

➤ I am embarrassed to promote myself and my work.

➤ I don't want people to think I am pushy or annoying.

➤ I can't brag about myself or my work.

➤ People don't appear interested.

➤ I hate selling.

There is no such thing as a good excuse.
Dero Ames Saunders

This exercise will empower you to succeed.

EXERCISE

It is very important that we become aware of our so-called shortcomings because then we can do something about them. As an exercise in confidence-building, rewrite your list making each of the preceding statements into a positive statement of strength. Don't worry that you don't believe it to be true at this moment. You will see when you do the exercise how easy it is to change your mindset. At the end of this writing exercise, you will feel that you can overcome your roadblocks. You will know that what is really holding you back is your attitude. A change of attitude is necessary and will empower you to succeed.

For example: "I never procrastinate."

_____

_____

_____

_____

_____

_____

_____

_____

_____

_____

_____

_____

The following list is the preceding 30 statements rewritten as statements of strength. It was put together by students from my *Art of Selling Art* seminars. This will help give you an idea of what I want you to do with your own list. First do the above exercise and then read over the following list.

➤ I never procrastinate.

➤ I am never afraid that I will be turned down or rejected.

➤ When it comes to selling, I'm great!

➤ I know what to say.

➤ I know how to approach a potential client.

➤ I'm always confident when making presentations.

➤ I know what questions to ask.

➤ My goals are clear, well-defined, and written down.

➤ I'm a skilled negotiator.

➤ I always know how to close.

➤ I always follow up.

➤ I know how to prospect effectively.

➤ I know how to use the telephone to conduct my business.

➤ I take control in any selling situation.

➤ I can be assertive when it is necessary.

➤ I have a strong and positive self-image.

➤ I have plenty of confidence.

➤ I have an organized sales approach.

➤ I'm highly motivated.

➤ I put my enthusiasm and energy into selling. I love it!

➤ I always find the time to sell because I know it is important.

➤ I have made the commitment to sell art.

➤ I always know my price and am not afraid to ask for it.

➤ I never allow fear of failure to stop me.

➤ I am an honorable and creative salesperson.

➤ I am proud to promote myself and my work.

➤ I am engaging and interesting.

➤ I am comfortable talking about myself and my work.

➤ I can tell when people are interested even when they try not to show it.

➤ I love to sell art.

THE PAYOFFS

Your personal reasons motivate your actions. Make a list below of all the reasons you want to sell art. Ask yourself the question, "Why do I want to sell art?" The more reasons you come up with, the better. Keep adding to your list as you continue your sales endeavors.

YOUR LIST OF PAYOFFS

Make a list below of all your reasons for selling art. The more reasons you list, the better. Add to your list daily.

_____
_____
_____
_____
_____
_____
_____
_____
_____
_____
_____
_____
_____
_____
_____
_____
_____
_____
_____
_____
_____

He who wishes to be rich in a day will be hanged in a year.
Leonardo da Vinci

28

SOME PAYOFFS

- Money
- Sharing
- Increased exposure
- To inspire excellence
- Personal satisfaction
- House improvements you've been wanting to make
- To feel validated
- Incentive to create more art
- To influence the world
- To add creative value to people's lives
- To promote a cause
- To support studio or gallery rent
- To increase public awareness
- Travel
- To inspire creative expression
- To increase the value of the artwork
- To raise self-esteem
- To be able to do what you love
- To add beauty to a working or living space
- Retirement savings

CHAPTER SUMMARY

❑ If you can create works of art, you can use your creativity to sell works of art.

❑ You must have a body of work (12-20 pieces that are completed) unified in theme, size and media.

❑ Your work must be unique to you, not a take-off on another artist.

❑ Show only your best work, no second-rate works.

❑ Be willing to let your works go.

❑ Create your work with selling in mind.

❑ Acknowledge your self-worth as an artist.

❑ Creating the right attitude is necessary and will make all the difference.

❑ It is your attitude much more than your aptitude that will determine your success.

❑ It doesn't cost anything to change your attitude.

❑ Do the exercises in this chapter, now!

Chapter 2
Why People Buy Art

Motivations

An ideal product

Our only limitations are those which we set up in our minds or permit others to establish for us. Elizabeth Arden

MOTIVATIONS

Understanding why a person wants to buy art is an important part of the sales process. People buy art because it brings them pleasure, happiness, joy, inspiration, satisfaction, prestige, etc. If you want to sell art, find out what brings these feeling to your clients and then help them own your artwork. They will be grateful.

It is *not* important what you like, but what your client likes. Put yourself mentally and emotionally into the client's space, try to get inside her wants and desires. Envision the rooms in her house or office space where the art will be hung or displayed. Go with what she wants, what she expresses liking.

Most people buy artwork because they like it.

➤ They connect to a work of art with their emotions.

➤ They like the feeling they get when they look at it.

➤ The art speaks to them in a personal way.

➤ They may also have respect and admiration for the artist and the labor that went into creating it.

➤ They may personally know and like the artist.

If you are convinced, you will be convincing.

Clients will, at times, ask you for your opinion about a work that they are admiring. Advise them according to your good and honest judgment. If you are convinced that the piece they are considering is right for them, advise them to buy it.

COLLECTING ART

Many people derive great joy from collecting art. They enjoy finding treasures while they are traveling in exotic places. They enjoy displaying these finds in their surroundings. Often when I visit people, I am given a tour of their art collection. The tour always includes the name of the artist for each piece and where it was purchased. People also receive satisfaction from donating art from their collections to the fine museums of the world.

Some people think that buying art is only for the wealthy. It is true that when some people reach a certain financial status, they think that they should begin buying some original art. One client said to me, "I don't know anything about buying art." I said, "Let's have lunch and I will educate you." You can help people make wise choices while purchasing art. Always be completely honest with

them, and they will be grateful to you and refer their friends to
you.

ART IS FOR EVERYONE

People buy art by well-known or emerging artists because they
want the pleasure of owning something that they really love, to
beautify their homes or add prestige to their office. People buy art
to enjoy it, to be inspired, and to feel good.

People spend their money for two basic reasons: to solve a problem
and to make them feel good. Art is purchased for the same two
reasons. People buy art for the same reasons they buy gourmet
food, luxury cars, beautiful clothes, and expensive homes. Art is a
solution to a problem—it is something to put on the wall or
display in the hall. Art also makes us feel good—it is a decorative
element in a home, office, school, church, hotel, or government
building.

But art is so much more. Generally, people buy art for the second
reason—good feelings. Art is a feel-good commodity. Art can also
enrich a person's life by adding spiritual nourishment and
inspiration. The value of an image can be far greater than the
money spent. Certain images are more valuable than gold to
people to transform consciousness, to create satisfaction and
happiness.

Art can also be a reminder of life's values. Art reminds people of
the things in life that are more important than money—family,
children, relationships, faith, values, passions or interests. Art
enriches people's lives like nothing else. Art can delight the heart
and mind. Art can remind people daily of their true value.

A SOLUTION TO A PROBLEM

Problem: One has to eat to stay alive.

Solution: One goes to the grocery store to buy food.

People buy cars because they need a fast and easy method of
transportation, clothes to stay warm and to protect them from the
elements, houses as shelter, doctors because they need medical

*Art is almost always
obtained because the buyer
feels some kind of personal
connection.*

attention, lawyers because they need legal assistance, architects to design buildings, tailors to alter clothes, and a cleaning service to clean offices or homes. All these services are made to resolve a problem.

TO FEEL GOOD

When people buy art, they choose that which is a reflection of their own personality.

Another reason people spend their money is to get a good feeling. They go to the grocery store to buy food that tastes good to them—food that they enjoy. They buy gourmet food or organic food even though it costs more because they are having guests for dinner and want to serve them the best. They want to share their good taste and prosperity with their friends. This gives them good feelings—feelings of generosity, satisfaction, happiness. They buy luxury cars because the looks and the extra functions of these cars make them feel important and successful. They also like to drive a well-built car because they expect to have trouble-free transportation. People buy beautifully-made expensive clothes to be well-dressed. They have their clothes tailored for a perfect fit to look their best and present themselves with elegant dignity in the social world. They can afford to dress well, so why not? People want to feel good about themselves, and beautiful clothes help them do that. People pay architects to design large, elegant homes for the same reasons. They want to feel good living in comfort and style and be able to entertain large groups of friends. They live in a country estate or an expensive neighborhood. It feels good to live like a king or queen. People hire plastic surgeons to look younger and feel better about themselves.

You can see how we often buy things for both reasons: They provide a solution to a problem and create a good feeling.

BUYING ART FOR INVESTMENT

People sometimes buy art for investment purposes. I do not recommend selling art for investment reasons. It is always great to hear that something you purchased 10 years ago is now worth 10 times what you paid for it. But who wants to live with something that he or she does not like, just because it might go up in value?

A friend of mine began buying art when he was very young and had little money. He would pick up original drawings, paintings and prints in a very low price range. In a few years, his apartment walls were covered with original works by many different artists. I'm sure that today some of these works are worth 10-100 times what he paid for them. But I'm also sure he would not part with his collection for the money. Most art is not bought for investment. Most people who buy art for investment spend a considerable sum of money on the piece because it has been created by an artist who is already well-known.

It is illegal in the state of Hawaii to sell art for investment purposes.

AN IDEAL PRODUCT

Many people think that art is hard to sell; of all the products on the market, it is one of the most difficult to move. If you were to look for an ideal product to sell, what would it be? What advantages would it have? What qualities?

EXERCISE I

Look at the list below and check all the qualities that you think apply to art. This will help you realize that art is an almost ideal product. It will help you appreciate what you are doing when you sell art.

❑ everyone wants/needs

❑ will last

❑ won't break

❑ is easy to produce

❑ enriches people's lives

❑ makes life easier

❑ will inspire excellence

❑ has a great profit spread

❑ improves with time

❑ you can collect

❑ all cultures value

❑ value is higher than price

❑ can't live without

❑ lifts a person's mood

❑ offers joy and peace

❑ cannot be duplicated

❑ will inspire creativity

❑ delights the heart/mind

❑ you can see before you buy

❑ will lead to more sales

❑ someone other than the artist can sell

❑ other people will respect you for owning

❑ feeds the soul—spiritual nourishment

❑ causes a person to crave more

❑ can generate future income

❑ is more valuable than gold

Owning art is prestigious.

EXERCISE II

Just for fun, go through the list again and check all the qualities
you think would apply to selling a BMW automobile. You
probably will find that art is a much more desirable product to sell.

_____   _____

_____   _____

_____   _____

_____   _____

_____   _____

_____   _____

_____   _____

_____   _____

_____   _____

EXERCISE III

Now go through the list again. If you can think of more
advantages, add them to the list. What are the qualities of the art
that you are selling? Keep these in mind when working with a
client. List them here.

_____   _____

_____   _____

_____   _____

_____   _____

_____   _____

_____   _____

_____   _____

_____   _____

_____   _____

CHAPTER SUMMARY

❑ People spend their money for two basic reasons: to solve a problem—to adorn a blank wall, to decorate a room, to enliven an interior space, to enhance an exterior landscape, to study an artist's work—or to make them feel good—the joy, the inspiration, the visual pleasure, the fun, the prestige.

❑ Most people buy art because it makes them feel good.

❑ Some people buy art to reflect their success and social status.

Chapter 3
Client Rapport

Attracting and keeping clients

Three-part formula

The handshake

The hidden dimension: distance

Tone of voice

Dress for success

Rapt attention is the highest form of flattery.   Anonymous

ATTRACTING AND KEEPING CLIENTS

As a salesperson, have your objective be not only to make sales but also to meet and keep clients. Remember, your clients are for a lifetime. If you have that attitude and treat them thus, that will become true. Each individual you meet is important and deserving of your highest regard. Treat everyone with dignity.

TELLING IS NOT SELLING

One of the most effective ways to complete a sale is to engage in a dialogue with the potential client in which you ask questions that will lead to a buying decision. Salespersons not trained in selling art usually try to tell their clients about the works they represent. My experience has taught me that clients might politely listen for a minute or so, but as the representative continues to talk, they become less and less interested. By telling, you will end up losing their attention and a sale.

People don't like to be told. They would rather tell you! The way to get your clients really interested in owning what you have to sell them—art—is to ask them questions, so that they can tell you their thoughts. The more they tell you, the more interested they will become.

A major part of success of living lies in the ability to put first things first. Indeed, the reason most major goals are not achieved is that we spend our time doing second things first.
Robert J McKain

Early one morning, when my son Michael was five years old, I discovered him waiting for me with his paintings displayed all over the dining room table. As I passed the table on my way to the kitchen to make breakfast, Michael stopped me and said, "Dad, I am selling these paintings. Which ones would you like?"

Well, not wanting to discourage my son, I stopped to admire his paintings. I selected two.

"I'll take this one and this one," I said, picking up the two paintings.

This is where he needed some training.

"How much will you give me for them?" he asked.

Always know your prices before you engage a client in a sales presentation.

Well, I thought, I'll take advantage of youth and inexperience. So I said to him, "How about 50 cents?"

"Only 50 cents!" he replied.

So then, feeling a little guilty, I said, "Then how about a dollar?"

Being only five years old, Michael thought that a dollar was considerably more than 50 cents and accepted my offer. So right there on the spot, I paid Michael the dollar and took possession of his artwork. With care and respect, I laid his artwork on my work table and proceeded to the kitchen to prepare breakfast. I thought we were finished. A few minutes later Michael came into the kitchen holding a small drawing in his hand. My little son came up to me and said, "Daddy, this is for you." And he handed me his small drawing. So, what did Michael do? He added something to the sale—something that I did not anticipate. He gave me more than I expected!

KEEPING CLIENTS

Which is more important, to make a single sale or to create loyal clients and collectors who will buy from you again and again? If you want to be successful selling art, give clients more than they expect to get. Gone are the days when you make a sale and the next day forget whom you sold to.

Get the idea that you are in the business of creating a base of clients who will buy from you again and again over many years. Your best clients will become good friends and loyal collectors. Also, your best clients will become your best publicity agents for finding new clients to increase your sales.

My son Michael teaches us one more lesson here. When Michael asked me to look at his display of paintings, he asked, "Which ones would you like?"

Even at five years old, he knew that he could probably sell me more than one just as easily as one. And he was right: I bought two! If he had said one, I would have selected one. Think volume sales rather than single sales. Think packages rather than one-of-a-kind.

Michael was entrepreneurial. He didn't have a gallery or a professional sales location. He didn't have a business card or a car. He used the dining room table. He was resourceful. Of course he had a willing client and he knew that. You, too, will have willing clients. Your parents and relatives can be very helpful. (My mom had a small antique shop. I used to wholesale my work to her, and she would resell it in her shop.) We must be open-minded and flexible. Learn to sell whenever and wherever you can—a client's home or office, home shows, sidewalk fairs, the local bank, restaurant, coffee shop, wherever the art happens to be. We need to take the art to our relatives and friends, just as Michael took his paintings to the dining room table and his dad.

It is wonderful if you have an elegant gallery space, but it is not necessary. A modest showroom or even a space that is rented for a weekend can inspire clients to buy. When they buy art in a low-rent showroom, they are not paying for the rental space. People always want to buy for less, as I did with Michael.

GIVING MORE THAN IS EXPECTED

When you sell something, make it a practice to give your clients something more than they expect. It could be a poster featuring the artist, a beautiful large postcard featuring one of the artist's works, or an invitation to a private showing with the artist. If you are an artist, the task is easy. You have all sorts of things around your studio that you could make into a thank-you gift for your clients. It could be a commemorative poster from a past show, a print, a small sketch, a book that features your works—something that your clients will appreciate having.

To be successful in the business of selling art, think of ways to develop a loyal clientele—collectors who will buy from you again and again. One way to do that is to give your clients more than they expect.

We can use a three-part formula to help us strengthen our client relationships. The stronger the rapport you have with a person, the more likely it is that he or she will want to do business with you. I call this formula the **ABC**'s of human relationships.

THREE-PART FORMULA

AFFECTION

A stands for affection. It means that you honestly care for another person. Affection is the genuine feeling of happiness to be with another person. If you find that this is difficult with some people, cultivate the attitude that there is always something you can pick out about another person that you can like. When people feel that you like them, they will likely return this affection. When people like you, they may be more open to your ideas. Always be polite to others. Make them feel important. If you do, you will have many good clients (and friends).

BEING IN AGREEMENT

B stands for being in agreement. The more agreement you have with a person, the more he or she will like you.

➤ The better you communicate, the more likely you will be to do business with the person. Ultimately, you want to agree that the sale is a good idea.

➤ Never, ever disagree or argue with a client. The client is always right.

➤ Use such phrases as, "That's right," "Good point," or "I see."

Client: "Wow, that is really expensive!"

Salesperson: "That's right! And it's worth it."

Each of the three ABC's is connected like the three sides of a triangle, and each needs to be kept strong.

COMMUNICATION

C stands for communication. This means the imparting or interchange of thoughts, opinions, or information between two or more people. With communication and the exchange of information, anything is possible. Pausing, listening, questioning, and telling a person you understand what has been said will promote good communication.

➤ It is important always to return telephone calls promptly.

➤ If you use e-mail, answer it daily.

➤ Always call before an appointment to verify the time.

When we are selling art, the degree of affection, level of agreement and quality of communication will either increase or decrease depending on what we say and ask and how we think, feel, and act in the presence of another person. These three conditions work together in harmony so that if one increases, they all increase. If one decreases, they all decrease. If you find that you are not in agreement, then you need to increase affection and improve communication. If communication is off, find agreement and increase affection.

In most sales situations, these ABC conditions are high when a sale is being made. After the sale is made, the level is even higher. Think of the process of selling art as both beneficial to the client and rewarding to you, with the bonus of cultivating some good friends and clients.

THE HANDSHAKE

Both men and women should have a good, firm handshake. Always begin and end your meeting with a new client (and all follow-up meetings) with a firm and friendly handshake. This is usually the first gesture between two people, and if it is not a strong beginning, your meeting will be off right from the start. When you meet art gallery representatives, also begin and end your meetings with a handshake. You often can tell how enthusiastic people are by the way they relate to you through their handshake.

➤ A handshake should be firm but not hard.

➤ It should be given with a warm smile.

➤ It should not be an uncomfortable squeeze.

➤ It should be short and to the point. Do not hold on. People who hold on to another person's hand may make that person feel uncomfortable. Sometimes people will do this as a way of holding your attention. If a client does this to you, it is best to grin and bear it. But don't do this to a client or gallery representative.

➤ A handshake should not communicate in any way that one person is superior to the other.

➤ Do not squeeze the other's fingers.

➤ Get a good grip of the entire hand, and if you don't get a good grip, do it over.

So much is communicated non-verbally with a handshake.

THE "WET FISH"

This is what we used to call a limp, soft handshake. If someone does this to you, you get the impression that the person is not really interested in having a strong connection, does not want to make a good impression or is indifferent. Some women do this because they think it is more gentle and feminine. It is not a good idea to do this. The "wet fish" communicates weakness of character.

THE POWER SQUEEZE

Some men like to show off their physical strength when shaking the hand of another man. It communicates superiority and the desire to dominate. It does not communicate sincerity and warmth but just the opposite. It communicates cold, hard domination. If you have a strong grip, be careful how you use it.

THE FINGER CRUSHER

This happens when someone squeezes the fingers of another. It is not a hand clasp but a finger crunch. The person on the receiving end feels put off and a little cheated. Sometimes it can happen when one clasps the other's hand too soon. (Try to be sure that the flesh between the thumbs and the first fingers is touching before the hands close.) When I get one of these handshakes, I say quickly, "Let's do that again." At the same time I gently take hold of the other person's wrist, release my hand and push it into the other person's hand quickly before he or she knows what's happening. That way we get a good handshake and start our meeting on a positive note.

THE DOMINANT/SUBORDINATE HANDSHAKE

This happens when one of the parties has his hand on top of the other person's. Usually he comes in for the handshake with a circular motion from above. His hand comes down onto the other person's. The dominant person has his hand on top of the subordinate person's. It is done quickly, and the non-verbal message is that the person with the hand on top is dominating. If someone does this to you, simply straighten out your hand so that the dominant hand will be vertical alongside your own.

THE FRIENDLY, WARM HANDSHAKE

The best handshake is the friendly, warm handshake, in which both parties clasp hands in a firm way. Both hands are vertical with their fingers pointing to the other person. The two clasps are equally firm, not squeezing, but firm. The shake is brief, friendly, and the two parties look each other in the eye and say, "How do you do?" or, "I'm very glad to meet you." Usually names are exchanged at the same time. It is the proper way today between two men, two women, or between a man and a woman.

There are many truths of which the full meaning cannot be realized until personal experience has brought it home.
John Stuart Mill

THE HIDDEN DIMENSION: DISTANCE

Physical distance can play an important role in your relationships. If one gets too close physically to another person, it can have a negative effect—the person may feel uncomfortable. Conversely, someone else may feel that the distance between you is too great to have meaningful communication. It is always important to find and feel the right psychological and physical distance for the other person.

The quality of your relationships will determine your success.

Let the other person determine the distance. Remain at that distance for the duration of your conversation. Sometimes, you might feel a little uncomfortable because the distance is too small or too large for your own comfort. Learn to accommodate your client.

When working in a gallery or studio space with clients, it is wise to be aware of spatial relationships between yourself and your clients. Americans have certain spatial envelopes that are comfortable in different situations. However, many foreigners operate in different spatial relationships. What I instruct my students to do is to allow the buyer to establish the distance that is comfortable. Then you, as the salesperson, stand firmly in that position even if it may feel awkward to you because it is either too far or too close for your personal comfort.

When two or more people are sharing the experience of viewing a painting or sculpture, the attention is on the art piece. In this situation, the physical distance between people can be quite close and at the same time comfortable. However, if you are facing a person and you are having a conversation, then the distance has to be a comfortable social distance. This distance can vary greatly in different cultures. Unless you are able to respect a person's cultural spatial comfort, you may find it difficult to establish and keep rapport.

This is an important consideration. You may find that a person will simply walk away and not realize why. Edward T. Hall found it so important that he wrote a book on the subject titled, *The Hidden Dimension,* first published in 1966. In his book, he outlined four principal categories of spatial relationships: intimate, personal, social, and public. His research showed that these distances are fairly constant in our American culture but vary considerably in foreign cultures.

Be mindful of spatial relationships.

The following chart shows Mr. Hall's four categories of measurements:

INTIMATE DISTANCE

Close phase: touching to 6"
Far phase: 6 - 18"

PERSONAL DISTANCE

Close phase: 1.5 - 2.5'
Far phase: 2.5 - 4'

SOCIAL DISTANCE

Close phase: 4 - 7'
Far phase: 7 - 12'

PUBLIC DISTANCE

Close phase: 12 - 25'
Far phase: 25'+

These distances differ considerably among cultures. The best distance for an American to maintain to conduct a discussion about art sales would be the Social Distance—Close phase. Of course the discussion might begin at the Social Distance—Far phase. At the Social Distance, the voice level is normal and both parties feel "safe."

EXERCISE

In order to become more aware, stand with a friend at different distances. Find the most comfortable distance to have a conversation and measure it with a tape measure. See how far away you can get without feeling awkward. Now try to stand closer. See how close you can get without feeling uncomfortable. Note that the distance is the same for both of you unless you are from different countries.

EXERCISE

Now stand together looking at an artwork. See how close you can stand side by side and feel comfortable. Measure the distance. You will see that there is quite a difference.

Man's feeling about being properly oriented in space runs deep. Such knowledge is ultimately linked to survival and sanity. To be disoriented in space is to be psychotic.
Edward T Hall

TONE OF VOICE

Your tone of voice has a profound influence on the mood and rapport that you will have with your clients. Ask your good friends to comment on your tone of voice. Do you speak too loudly or too softly? Does your voice sound harsh? Do you speak too fast or too slowly?

Controlling your voice is very important. Learn to use it to your advantage.

Learn to be aware of the tone of voice you usually use. Find out if it has the effect of making people feel relaxed. One way to become more aware of this is to set up a tape recorder and record conversations with a friend. Play it back, listening to your voice.

SPEED OF SPEAKING

When you are working with a client, match the tone of voice and the speed of speaking that your client is using. This will help your client feel at ease with you. When you are speaking to a client on the telephone, do the same. Remember, the more rapport you have with a person, the more likely the person will want to buy from you. Match his speed and tone of voice. Practice this when you speak on the phone with anyone, and soon you will be in the habit of matching tone and speed for all your business conversations.

DRESS FOR SUCCESS

A gallery show or reception can be an opportunity to put on a little flair. Use color and have some fun with style. Look good, feel confident, and you will meet and connect with people easily.

Potential clients form their impression of you in the first instant after meeting you. You will never get a second chance to make this first impression. How you appear will have a strong effect on whether they want to do business with you. How they look is not important. What matters is how you look. Do you look like a person who will be selling a work of art? Do you look like you know what you are doing?

FOR THE ARTIST

Wearing your painting or sculpting attire may not be a good way to present yourself to a potential buyer. Many people have difficulty relating to another person who is dressed radically differently from themselves. Remember that your goal is to gain rapport. Dress in a way that will help your clients feel comfortable. Look like a professional. The way you dress can either put another person off or make him feel good to be with you. Forget your own comfort and dress the part. Make sure that your hands and fingernails are clean. Most people will feel more comfortable shaking a clean hand.

MEN

Men should wear a suit or sport coat. On the East Coast, a neck tie is a must. On the West Coast, dress tends to be a little more casual, and an open neck is sometimes acceptable. In Hawaii, the dress is even more casual and men can sometimes look appropriately attired in a beautiful aloha shirt. Men should always wear neatly pressed long trousers with a belt—never shorts or jeans. Your hair and/or mustache and beard should be neat and trimmed. Always wear socks and shined shoes. In tropical climates, good-looking sandals may be worn with socks.

WOMEN

Women should wear business attire. Scarves and other accessories can add flair and color. Women's hair should be well groomed and neat. Keep shoes clean and shined, and only wear sandals or open-toed shoes if they look professional on you.

People will not tell you if they don't approve of or appreciate the way you look. You must be self-aware and make yourself look the part that you have chosen to play. If you want to be financially successful, dress like you already are successful. Dressing well can help you feel good inside. You will have more confidence because you know you look great.

❏ Think volume sales rather than single sales. Think packages rather than one-of-a-kind.

❏ Learn to sell whenever and wherever you can—wherever the art happens to be.

❏ When selling art, remain open-minded and resourceful.

❏ Orient your thinking to ways to develop a loyal clientele—collectors who will buy from you again and again. One way to do that is to give your clients more than they expect.

❏ People's emotions are a more powerful motivator to buy than their reason.

❏ Learn what questions to ask to involve your client emotionally.

❏ It is much easier to connect with your clients emotionally than to try to help them overcome their objections. When people really want to own a work, they will overcome their own objections.

❏ People need good reasons to help rationalize spending their money. Provide reasons.

❏ The ABC of human relationships will determine your degree of rapport. The more rapport you have with a client, the better your chances of making a sale.

❏ Always be polite to others and make them feel that they are important. If you do this, you will have many good clients as well as return clients.

❏ If you don't have a good handshake, practice until you get in the habit of giving a good, firm handshake.

❏ Begin and end all meetings with a good handshake.

CHAPTER SUMMARY

❑ Use good eye contact with your clients, but don't stare them down.

❑ Let the buyer establish the distance that is comfortable. Then you, as the salesperson, stand firm in that position even if it may feel awkward.

❑ Ask friends to comment on your tone of voice.

❑ Tape-record your voice during a real conversation.

❑ Match your speed of speaking and tone of voice to your client's, practicing on the phone and in everyday conversations.

Chapter 4
Sales Skills

The four skill levels

The elevator to success is out of order. You'll have to use the stairs, one step at a time. Joe Girard

FOUR SKILL LEVELS

There are four stages to learning a new skill:

UNCONSCIOUSLY UNSKILLED

When you began reading this book, you may not have had much of an idea about what was involved in the selling of art. This is the beginning level. Think about learning to sell the same way you would think about learning to drive a car. I call it a skill you can learn. Remember when you didn't know anything about driving a car? I call this level "unconsciously unskilled."

CONSCIOUSLY UNSKILLED

The second level is when you have some idea about what you need to learn to master the skill (in this case, sales). Let's say you have read this book, but that is all. Reading alone will not help you much. You have to make a commitment to put the information you have read to use—to actually practice what is recommended. You can read the driving manual as much as you want, but until you get behind the wheel of a car and practice driving, you will not know how to drive.

CONSCIOUSLY SKILLED

The third level is becoming consciously skilled. This is the stage when you begin to practice selling art. At each stage of this part of the process, you have to think, think, think. What is next? Am I doing this right? What question should I ask now? Which question should I ask to close? When you learned to drive, you had to remember how to turn a corner, to signal a turn, to watch your speed, to stop at stop signs, etc. You knew if you did not remember these things, you would fail the driving test. You had to remain alert and conscious about everything you did. The same goes for sales at this level of skill.

UNCONSCIOUSLY SKILLED

Expect to sell.

When you become unconsciously skilled, you have graduated to the fourth and final level. At this stage, you have practiced so many times that what you say and do during a sale has become second nature. You will have developed your own methods of gentle selling, which incorporate suggestions in this book.

➤ You automatically ask questions and listen; you involve your clients in the works of art you are selling by asking them questions.

➤ You know how to find out what they want.

➤ You know how to test and close your sales (Chapter 9).

➤ You routinely ask for referrals.

➤ You have a great vocabulary and never use emotionally-loaded words.

➤ You build rapport with your clients so that they keep coming back to you.

You will learn all these methods in this book. They will become second nature, just as when you drive a car now, you can listen to the radio, carry on a conversation, and still automatically stop, signal, turn, watch your speed, and drive safely without giving it much thought.

The best way to get good at selling art is to practice selling art. When you have done it for a year or two, you will be at the fourth level.

CHAPTER SUMMARY

❑ There are four skill levels in selling art. You are unconsciously unskilled at the first level. You don't know what you don't know.

❑ The second level is when you become consciously unskilled. You know what you need to learn.

❑ The third level is becoming consciously skilled. You need to consciously think at each step of the process.

❑ The fourth level is becoming unconsciously skilled. You are very practiced, and you move through each step of the process with ease and confidence. Your skill is almost automatic—you can perform appropriately without much thought.

❑ The best way to get to the fourth level in selling art is to practice selling art!

Chapter 5
Word Power

14 power words

Negative words

Increasing your vocabulary

Describing colors

Describing artists

Everything depends upon execution; having just a vision is no solution.
Stephen Sondheim

14 POWER WORDS

Listed below are 14 power words to remember to use when you are selling art. Use them in conversations with clients as well as when writing promotional material for press releases or publicity announcements. These words attract curiosity, create interest, inspire imagination and motivate action.

BEST

DISCOVER

EASY

GUARANTEED

LOVE

MONEY

NEW

OWN

PROVEN

SAFE

SAVE

TRUST

VALUE

YOU

DESCRIPTIVE FORMAT

Following are sample sentences using these 14 power words.

BEST

You can be assured that you are acquiring the best.

In the field of modern impressionists, she is one of the best.

This is the best price for these that you will find anywhere.

DISCOVER

This artist's work has just been discovered.

Discover the power in this artist's paintings.

I want you to discover how easy it is to own this artist's work.

EASY

With these prices, it is easy to own the work.

The style is easy to like.

The artist's painting style is easy to understand and captivating.

GUARANTEED

These bronzes are guaranteed to last for thousands of years.

These prints are guaranteed to delight any discriminating collector.

These paintings are guaranteed to add _____ to your life.

LOVE

When you fall in love with a work, you just have to own it.

You will love this artist's new work.

I just love the wild colors in this painting.

MONEY

When you purchase a piece during this show, you will save money.

If you would like to save money, we can offer you a discount if you buy more than one print at a time.

NEW

We are featuring new work by _____.

These new paintings (sculptures, prints) are the subject of this special exhibition.

His recent work addresses a new theme in his painting.

OWN

When you see these new works, you will want to own them all.

Just think what it would be like to own an original _____.

PROVEN

His work has proven to be the most popular with our clients.

Our reputation for quality art and service has been proven by our 25 years in business as a highly regarded art gallery.

SAFE

When you buy from our gallery, you have the safety of knowing that we will live up to our fine reputation for care and trustworthiness.

You can be sure that we do not hold back on the framing; we need to insure the safety of the piece.

SAVE

By deciding today, we can save you the cost of framing and shipping.

Our art consulting service can save you hours of shopping time.

When you purchase more than one piece, you can save money with valuable discounts.

TRUST

You can trust that we have a reputation to uphold and we operate our gallery with the highest integrity.

You can trust this is an authentic original.

VALUE

These original prints are a great value because the artist is still relatively unknown.

You and your family will value this piece for many years to come.

The piece has exceptional value.

YOU

You will love the power and magnificence in this work.

You will want to own an original _____.

I knew that her work would appeal to you.

QUESTION FORMAT

Now let's demonstrate how these words can be used in interrogative sentences. I've taken the preceding sentences and made them into questions. In the question format, these words are even more effective.

BEST

You would like to be assured that you are acquiring the best, wouldn't you?

Do you know that in the field of the modern impressionists, she is one of the best?

Do you know that this is the best price for these that you will find anywhere?

DISCOVER

Can you imagine that this artist's work has just been discovered?

Would you like to discover how easy it is to love and own this new artist's work?

EASY

With these prices, it is easy to own the work; don't you agree?

It is a style that is easy to like, isn't it?

Can you see how this artist's direct painting style is easy to understand and is still captivating?

GUARANTEED

Did you know that we guarantee that these bronzes will last for at least a thousand years?

Don't you agree that these prints are guaranteed to delight any discriminating collector?

Did you know that everything in the gallery is guaranteed to be authentic?

LOVE

When you fall in love with a work, you just have to own it; don't you agree?

Don't you love this artist's new work?

Don't you just love the wild colors in this painting?

MONEY

Do you know that when you purchase a piece during this show, you are going to save money?

Do you know that if you buy more than one of these prints at a time, you will save considerable money?

NEW

Would you like to see the new work we are featuring by _____?

Do you see how this recent work addresses a new theme?

OWN

When you see these new works, you want to own them all, don't you?

Can you imagine what it would be like to own an original _____?

PROVEN

I'm sure you are not surprised that his work has proven to be the most popular with our clients, are you?

Do you know that we are a highly regarded art gallery proven by 25 years in the art business?

SAFE

You know when you purchase art from our gallery, you have the safety of knowing that we will live up to our fine reputation for care and trustworthiness, don't you?

You can be sure we will frame the piece properly; we need to insure the safety of the piece, don't we?

SAVE

Would you like to save the cost of framing and shipping?

Would you like to learn how our art consulting service can save you hours of shopping time and money with valuable discounts?

TRUST

Can you trust that we have a reputation to uphold and that we operate our gallery with the highest integrity?

You know you can trust that this is an authentic original, don't you?

VALUE

Don't you agree that these original prints are a great value?

Can you imagine how you and your family will value this piece for many years to come?

Can you see the exceptional value here?

YOU

Don't you love the power and magnificence in this work?

Wouldn't you like to own an original _____?

Her work appeals to you, doesn't it?

Can you see how using these 14 words in a question format will increase communication and agreement?

NEGATIVE WORDS

When selling art, you should avoid certain words. These words are negatively charged and will, in many cases, cause a client to feel uneasy or uncomfortable—just the opposite of what you want. We want our clients to feel relaxed and comfortable while they are making decisions to own art. Word choice and tone of voice will help keep your clients feeling at ease. Following are nine emotionally-loaded words to avoid, with some suggestions for substitutes.

BUY

acquire	collect	have
invest	obtain	own
take	add to your collection	
opportunity to own		

CONTRACT

agreement	paperwork

COST OR PRICE

available for	being offered at	goes for
monthly investment	ranges	total investment
valued at	worth	

CUSTOMER

client	colleague	collector
friend	patron	

DEAL

opportunity

DOWN PAYMENT OR DEPOSIT

initial investment	put something down

PITCH

demonstration	presentation

SELL OR SELLING

distribute	exhibit	letting it go
make available	market	offer
place	present	promote
provide	represent	show

SIGN

approve	authorize it	endorse it
okay it	complete the paperwork	

"Own" has the connotation of gaining something. "Buy" has the connotation of losing something.

When you are talking with clients in a gallery or at an opening, it is important to have a good vocabulary to describe the works of art and the artists. The more colorful the words you use, the more impressive your descriptions will be. Too often I hear people describe art and they use only one or two words—"interesting" or "nice." Refrain from using either word. The word "interesting" doesn't communicate much more than, "I don't know what else to say." The word "nice" communicates, "I just want to say something positive."

When speaking about a specific work, find the right words to describe how you feel and what you see. When you need to write press releases, artist's statements, or reviews about artwork, it is helpful to have a strong art vocabulary. Use the following lists of words as a resource. Add to the list other words that you find appropriate. These words will help you create impressive statements about the art, the artist you represent, and the colors you see.

EXERCISE

Write a one-sentence description of the art you are selling using the lists on the next two pages. Use at least one word from the first, second, third and fourth columns. You will see how easy it is to come up with a strong, descriptive statement. Give it a try.

INCREASING YOUR VOCABULARY

DESCRIPTIVE WORDS FOR ARTWORKS

admired	aesthetic	alive	amusing
appealing	articulated	acerbic	attractive
available	awesome	basic	bitter
breakthrough	bright	brilliant	busy
calm	captivating	charming	classic
classy	clever	clean	creative
collectable	colorful	commanding	compelling
contemporary	contrasting	conversation piece	
contoured	cool	cozy	current
dark	dazzling	delectable	delicate
delicious	delightful	depth	detail
dominating	dramatic	dreamlike	dynamic
dynamite	earthy	easy	electric
elegant	elite	energetic	enigmatic
ethereal	esthetic	evocative	explosive
exquisite	extraordinary	fascinating	fancy
fantasy	fiery	finely crafted	flavor
flowing	free	freedom	fresh
fun	glorious	glowing	gorgeous
graceful	great	handsome	harmonious
human	humorous	iconographic	imaginative
important	influential	ingenious	innovative
inspiring	intelligent	intense	intricate
inventive	keen	latest	lifelike
light	limited edition	lucid	liquid
lovely	luminous	magical	magnetic
magnificent	masterful	masterpiece	melodious

Do what you love, love what you do, and deliver more than you promise.
Harvey Mackay

metaphysical   moving   museum-quality

musical   new   naïve   natural

organic   original   ornate   otherworldly

outstanding   painterly   passionate   perfect

playful   potent   powerful   precious

presence   primitive   quiet   rare

recent   respected   restful   revolutionary

rhythmic   rubbery   serene   sharp

shine   smart   soft   spicy

spiritual   splendid   spontaneous   striking

strong   stunning   sweet   tasteful

tempting   textured   tour de force   traditional

treasured   up-to-date   valuable   valued

vibrant   vigorous   vital   warm

weird   well-regarded   witty   whimsical

wonderful

DESCRIBING COLORS

It is important to have a good color vocabulary because it will

➤ Expand your own ability to see and appreciate color.

➤ Make you more knowledgeable as a professional.

➤ Give you a more accurate and distinctive vocabulary.

➤ Help you discuss the subtleties of color.

➤ Help you educate and expand your clients' knowledge of color.

Looking for just the right name for a color? The following list will give you some suggestions. Some of the colors listed are the names of colors on tubes of oil paint, acrylic paint and watercolor that will be familiar to artists. Add your own colors to this list.

EXERCISE

Write a descriptive statement about a real art piece that you represent, using the previous list and some of the colors from the following pages.

_____

_____

_____

_____

_____

_____

_____

_____

_____

_____

_____

_____

_____

DESCRIPTIVE WORDS FOR COLORS

alabaster	alizarin crimson	almond	amber
amethyst	antique gold	apricot	aquamarine
auburn	aureolin	azure	basic black
beige	blond	blue	blue violet
blue-black	brilliant white	bronze	brown
buff	burgundy	burnt orange	burnt sienna
burnt umber	cadmium orange	cadmium red	canary yellow
caramel	cerise	cerulean blue	chartreuse
Chinese red	chocolate	cinnabar	coal black
cobalt blue	cobalt green	colorless	copper
coral	cream	crimson	cyan
deep red	deep . . . etc.	dioxazine purple	
ebony	ecru	emerald	emerald green
flake white	flame red	flaxen	flesh
flesh tone	forest green	full spectrum	geranium
gold	goldenrod	grape	grass green
gray	ice blue	Indian red	indigo
iridescent gold	iridescent white	iridescent . . . etc.	
ivory	ivory black	ivory white	jade
jet black	lamp black	lavender	leaf green
lemon yellow	light yellow	lilac	lime
luminous gold	luminous green	luminous orange	luminous, etc.
magenta	mahogany	marigold	marine blue
mars black	mauve	midnight black	midnight blue
mint green	mistletoe	Naples yellow	navy
navy blue	neutral grey	off-white	olive

olive green	orchid	peach	peacock blue
pearl	pearl white	pewter	pink
plum	Prussian blue	Prussian green	pumpkin
pure white	radiant gold, yellow, etc.		raven black
raw sienna	raw umber	reddish . . . etc.	reddish purple
reddish violet	rose	ruby	russet
rust	salmon	sandy	sap green
sapphire	scarlet	scarlet lake	sepia
shocking pink	sienna	silver	sky blue
smoky gray	spring green	straw	sunset orange
tan	tangerine	taupe	tawny
terra verte	turquoise	turquoise blue	ultramarine
ultramarine blue	umber	Van Dyck brown	
Venetian red	vermilion	violet	viridian
viridian green	white	whiter-than-white	
winter white	yellow ochre	zinc white	

DESCRIBING ARTISTS

When you are talking to clients, or writing a biography, it is important to have a good vocabulary to describe yourself or the artist you represent. Artists can be colorful and fascinating characters. The more vivid the words you use, the more impressive your descriptions will be.

When you write about yourself or the artist you represent for a press release or a biographical statement, the list below will give you ideas to make your written statement more exciting to read.

EXERCISE

Write a sentence describing an artist, using at least three words from the following list. If it is about yourself, write the sentence in the third person.

Example: "Pablo Picasso, a robust, clever and dedicated artist while he was alive, produced a huge body of imaginative and masterful drawings, prints, paintings, and sculpture that have won the respect of collectors of modern art worldwide."

DESCRIPTIVE WORDS

able	accurate	adept	admired
adroit	alert	ambitious	amusing
appreciated	articulate	artistic	authoritative
aware	bright	brilliant	brave
bold	calm	capable	careful
celebrated	charming	clever	commanding
compassionate	competent	confident	conscious
consistent	contemporary	controlled	creative
current	decisive	dedicated	demanding
detail-oriented	devoted	dominant	dominating
emerging	energetic	enlightened	entertaining
enthusiastic	established	esteemed	experienced

We don't see things as they are, we see them as we are.
Anais Nin

expert — fine craftsman — foreign — fresh voice

friendly — gifted — great — hardworking

honest — honored — humane — humorous

imaginative — individualistic — influential — ingenious

inspired — integrity — intelligent — intellectual

inventive — keen — known — loved

magnetic personality — major — masterful

modern — most imitated — motivated — mysterious

national treasure — new — outstanding — passionate

played a major role — potent force — powerful

practiced — prolific — prominent — quick-witted

recent — reliable — renowned — resourceful

respected — revered — risk-taker — robust

scholarly — seasoned — sharp — simple

skillful — smart — sophisticated — spontaneous

straightforward — successful — timely — trained

treasured — truthful — up-to-date — valued

veteran — vigorous — weird — well-known

well-regarded — witty — won the respect of . . .

wonderful — worldly

❑ Use the following words—best, discover, easy, guaranteed, love, money, new, own, proven, safe, save, trust, value, you—when you write about or discuss art with your clients.

❑ Use the above words when you write promotional or publicity materials.

❑ Remember that these powerful words attract curiosity, create interest, inspire imagination, and motivate action.

❑ The words you use will influence the degree of comfort your client experiences when making a buying decision. Here is a quick reference of substitute words. Make using these substitute words a habit.

- sell or selling—offer or offering

- buy—own

- cost or price—value

- contract—paperwork

- pitch—presentation

- customer—client

- deal—opportunity

- sign—endorse

- down payment or deposit—put something down

❑ Invent your own creative way of offering art. For example, you could say, "Would you like this piece to come live with you?"

CHAPTER SUMMARY

Chapter 6
Phone Power

Using the phone

Making sales calls

Knowing is not enough; we must apply. Willing is not enough; we must do.
Johann von Goethe

USING THE PHONE

The telephone is an important tool in the selling process. I have sold art over the phone to people who have seen the art but have never met me. It hasn't happened often. Usually you will need to make face-to-face contact with your client before a sale takes place. Your comfort and skill on the phone can greatly enhance the effectiveness of your efforts to get appointments and close sales. Each time you talk on the phone, whether it is to a client or a friend, practice some of the following suggestions to develop good telephone skills.

A VOICE PICTURE

Remember that the inflection and tone in your voice communicate. What we say with words is only part of the message. When we talk on the phone with a stranger, we get a visual picture of the person from her voice—a voice picture. If your voice sounds upbeat, strong, clear and confident, the person you are talking with will receive a good impression.

Be sure to speak distinctly. Don't talk too fast or slur your words. Phone connections, especially on cellular phones, can be unclear. You might not know how your voice is being heard on the other end. You may hear your client perfectly, but the client may be having difficulty hearing you.

ANSWERING THE PHONE

When you answer the phone, say the name of your company and then give your first name or your first and last name.

"Contemporary Art Gallery, this is Rick Smith."

If you are an artist answering the phone, you may want to say just your last name or your first name instead of, "Hello." I answer my phone by saying, "This is Robert," with an upbeat tone at the end. I have at times just said my last name. I don't say, "Hello." "Hello" doesn't sound businesslike.

Be sure to answer the phone distinctly. If you have employees, coach them on good phone techniques. My office assistant answers my phone with, "Robert Dvořák's studio, this is Laura." Have your employees read this section of the book, and then practice with them. So many times when I called an office and the person gave his name, I couldn't understand what it was. I then had to ask the person to repeat it. I always want to know at least the first name of the person I am talking to. I have learned that if the person on the phone knows that you care enough to identify him by name, that person will likely be more courteous and helpful.

When speaking on the phone, use the person's name during the conversation. This will help increase your rapport with the other speaker. Sound upbeat and sincere. Sound like you are glad to be having this conversation. Ask your friends how you sound on the phone. Ask them to give you an honest assessment. Then work to correct any poor habits you may have.

When you answer a business call, always acknowledge the caller's interest and use the caller's name.

Salesperson: "Thank you for calling about the large painting in the gallery show, Judy."

or

Salesperson: "I'm pleased you want to come for a studio visit, Bill. Would Tuesday afternoon at 3:00 work for you, or would Wednesday at 10:00AM be better?"

➤ When possible, answer with a question that will lead to an appointment.

➤ When making an appointment, confirm all the details.

➤ Be sure to verify with a phone call the day of the appointment.

PHONE LOGS

Have a telephone log next to your phone. I use a three-ring binder that I keep open. It is filled with blank pages, and I make notes in it while I am talking on the phone and after the call is complete. It is a good idea to date each page; that way you can keep track of all your calls and the information is always available in one place. You won't have to look around for scattered papers to find information. It becomes a time-saver as well as an organizer. When you use a phone log, you will be able to refer to all the details of your conversations.

The most important single ingredient in the formula of success is knowing how to get along with people.
Theodore Roosevelt

Your clients will feel important when they realize that you are interested and organized on their behalf. When I travel between my home and my studio, I carry my phone log with me so that I always have it wherever I am.

OUT GOING PHONE MESSAGES

If you are an artist, you probably don't appreciate interruptions during your creative work sessions. Don't let the telephone run your life; let your answering machine take your calls while you are working. Put a short message on your answering machine. As an artist, you may want to do something clever or creative. I have an artist friend whose message is, "The time is NOW! Please leave a message." Don't add a musical background or your child's voice to the message on your business phone. This is unprofessional. Keep your message straightforward and simple.

My own message is, "This is Robert's studio phone. Please leave your name and number slowly and distinctly. And thank you for calling." I put an up-tone at the end of the last statement. It is a friendly message and makes an important request. People know their own phone numbers so well that they often say them too fast. Sometimes it is difficult to understand each number. When I leave my phone number, I always say it slowly and distinctly.

Every time you make a call, look at it as a training exercise. Do the best job you can, and you will do better every time.

LEAVING A MESSAGE

When leaving a message, give your number at the beginning of the message and again at the end. Always leave your number, even if you know that the person has it. You will be more likely to get a fast callback if you leave your number, and it is much easier for the recipient.

SMILE

Answer and talk on the phone with a smile. Put a mirror in front of your telephone to help you remember this. When you smile, you sound more friendly. A friendly disposition and tone of voice help people relax and feel good, and they will like you.

STAND

If you are making an important call or a call in which you want to sound confident and strong, standing while you are talking may help. It increases your energy level and gives your voice more power.

Be perceptive and listen to the tone of the other speaker's voice. If she sounds like she is busy and really doesn't want to talk to you right then, ask when a good time to call back would be. Suggest *two* times. This consideration will be appreciated. When you call back, the person will be more inclined to talk to you.

Salesperson: "It sounds like you are in the middle of something, Bill. I can call you back later this afternoon or the first thing in the morning. Which would be better for you?"

SCRIPT IMPORTANT CALLS

It is helpful to script your important telephone calls. Write out what you are going to say and the anticipated answers. Try to think of all the possible responses and script out your follow-up statements. Practice your script with a friend on the phone before making the call. This will give you the confidence you need when you make the actual call.

EXERCISE

Write a script for a call you want to make but, up to now, have been procrastinating because you don't want to be turned down or embarrassed. Practice the script with a friend a number of times. Make adjustments in your script. Then make the call and write the result in your phone log. Record all the information you need.

_____

_____

_____

_____

_____

_____

_____

_____

_____

MAKING SALES CALLS

TIP

The best time to make a sales call is mid-morning after 10:00AM. People generally feel better and fresher and more receptive after they have had their coffee or tea. After lunch, a lot of people feel sluggish. Near the end of the day, many people get tired and are less receptive.

WARM CALLS

The easiest calls to make are what I call warm calls. These are calls that follow up a chance meeting you had, a referral, or an inquiry on your answering machine. A call that follows up an earlier meeting will give you a better chance for getting an appointment.

➤ Be flexible. Go to them if they can't or don't seem willing to come to you.

➤ Be sure that when you schedule a meeting, the decision-maker will be present.

➤ If it is a couple, be sure that both parties will be present.

➤ Be prepared to handle objections to setting up a meeting.

➤ Answer questions and then ask a question.

➤ Use questions to move the call along quickly to an appointment. Your client will appreciate your efficiency.

❑ Speak clearly, distinctly, and with an upbeat tone of voice.

❑ Smile when talking on the phone.

❑ Always use the person's name during the conversation.

❑ Be polite and sincere. Never argue, lose your temper, sound impatient or say something sarcastic.

❑ Script your important calls.

❑ Ask questions to move the call along quickly to an appointment.

❑ Keep a log of each sales call you make. Write down all the information you can while you are talking, and fill in details immediately after the call is completed.

❑ Enter all appointments in your calendar immediately.

❑ Follow up with a reminder call the day of the appointment.

CHAPTER SUMMARY

Chapter 7
Listening Power

It's good to shut up sometimes.   Marcel Marceau

ASK QUESTIONS

Selling is a question and answer process.

Questions are the vitality of the selling process.

➤ Always clarify what is being said with questions.

➤ Never assume that you know what the other person wants or means.

➤ Never say, "I know exactly the kind of thing you are looking for." Rather, ask your clients to be very specific in regard to what they like and what they want.

Client: "I really like what those swirling colors do to me!"

Salesperson: "What do you mean, exactly?"

The question, "What do you mean, exactly?" is a great question to remember and use. It asks the client to elaborate on the statement. It lets the client know that you are really interested in the idea.

As a salesperson, you want to say the right things, but it is more important to hear what the other person is saying. Listen attentively to your client and then you will be able to respond appropriately. If you are always thinking what to ask or say next, you will not hear your clients' ideas.

QUALIFYING

Early in your conversation with a potential client, it is good to learn more about the client's ability to pay for the art he or she is admiring. You learn this through the questions you ask and the answers you receive.

Much information can be learned through casual conversation, as well as clues such as clothing and jewelry—although these are not always dependable. Often you will find a more eccentric client who may look casual or even scruffy but is worth many millions.

Let your questions be subtle and flow freely in normal conversation. You may learn that they belong to a country club, are the owners of their company, live in a large house in an upscale neighborhood, or own a luxury car. All of these facts can be indicators that they like luxury and are not afraid to spend their money for something that they really want. One of my favorite questions is, "Do you collect art?"

If they do, they will be proud to tell you so. And if they don't volunteer to tell you what they already have, you can ask:

"May I ask what you already own?"

When they tell you, ask:

"Would you like to find something that complements your current collection or would you like to find something that will be new and original?"

Of course, this is an alternative of choice question. Any affirmative answer implies that they would like to find something. If the clients tell you that they have never bought an original piece of art before, then you can ask:

"Are you open to beginning an art collection today?"

On occasion you may meet a person who is looking for new art. A collector who is a connoisseur of art prides himself on discovering emerging artists. If you encounter this kind of collector, you have an opportunity to introduce the newest and most unusual art that you have available. Ask:

Salesperson: "Do you have a budget?"

Client: "Why yes, I never purchase any piece for more than $5,000."

Salesperson: "Great, then I know to show you only works that are available for $5,000 or less."

Whether your clients buy from you or not, before they leave, be sure to ask them:

"May I contact you with future opportunities that I feel you would appreciate?"

"May we include you on our gallery mailing list?"

"Do you have a good friend that you know would appreciate being on our mailing list?"

Sometimes you will meet people who tell you that they are not in a position to spend any money on art, even though they love what they are seeing. Be sure to let them know that you will be ready to work with them when they are ready to begin collecting. Follow up by asking them if they have friends who collect and would benefit from your services.

Find out:
- *Name, address, phone*
- *Net worth*
- *Annual income*
- *Do they already collect art? If so, what do they own?*
- *Travel experience—do they take cruises or look for budget travel packages?*
- *What would inspire them to make a buying decision?*

LISTEN

Questions empower you. But only ask questions your client is capable of answering. If you ask a question a client cannot answer, your clients may feel stupid. If you make your clients feel stupid, they won't like you, and your ability to communicate will be lessened. Be attentive and ask the right questions to help your clients make the right buying decisions that they will be happy with for years to come.

➤ It is with questions that you test close and close the sale. With questions you are able to get referrals after the sale is complete.

➤ Never tell when you can ask.

➤ Never talk when you can listen. When you tell people something, they may doubt you, but if they tell you something, they believe it is true.

THE RIGHT QUESTIONS

The most intelligent strategy the art salesperson can use is to ask the right questions and listen carefully to the answers. Begin by asking general questions and as you learn more, make your questions more and more specific. Always ask for clarification. If there is anything at all that your client says that you don't understand, say, "What do you mean, exactly?"

Client: "I really like the subterfuge in that painting."

Salesperson: "What do you mean, exactly?"

Client: "I mean, I really like the way the artist uses the imagery to create mystery and deception. I like art that goes deeper than the obvious."

Salesperson: "Yes, this painting has some powerful imagery that goes beyond the obvious. It kind of grabs you and pulls you in, don't you agree?"

I think you can see how a conversation like this will help you to connect the person to the work. If you had just said, "Uh huh," where would you be? By asking for clarification, you slow down the conversation, increase clarity, and at the same time build trust and rapport.

It is better to know some of the questions than all of the answers.
James Thurber

THE PRIME FACTOR

The prime factor is the most important concern to your client. It is a specific problem, a particular need, something of great interest, or a love or passion. A prime factor can motivate a person to make a buying decision. If you can find out what a person's prime factor is, you can lead the person to making a beneficial decision. Let your clients talk! Ask open-ended questions, and listen. When people ask you very specific questions and you offer specific details, you are really connecting with them.

If a new client shares information and asks questions about a work of art, you can be certain that the person is interested in learning more about the piece or the artist. One way to discover if you have found a prime factor is to watch a person's body language. If a person changes his posture suddenly, or starts taking notes or asking a lot of questions, you have probably found their prime factor. Once you think that you have found it, stay with it, ask more questions about it, and try to connect the person's interest with her prime factor.

When you ask questions and listen, you gain trust.

Client: "We have just moved our office to a new space. It is much larger and we would like to hang some fabulous art on the new walls."

Salesperson: "Can you describe the walls?" (listen to the answer)

"How large are they?" (listen to the answer)

"How high are the ceilings?" (listen to the answer)

"Are the walls painted white?" (listen to the answer)

Salesperson: "Why don't I meet you at your office space tomorrow to check out the space? I will bring a few works with me and we can see how they enhance the space. Would 10:00AM be a good time for you? Or would the afternoon be better, say 2PM?"

Here, the client shared with the sales representative the prime factor—looking for artwork to enhance the work space. This is a real need, and a real opportunity for you as a salesperson. You will want to work closely with this client. Visit the space. Show the client artwork to learn about his taste in art. Notice at the end of

Build rapport by being genuinely interested in your clients' needs. Show your clients that you will go out of your way to satisfy their desires.

the dialogue above that there is a suggestion and a question. The suggestion is to visit the office space with some works of art. Then the question follows, asking the client to make a choice between two times. When the client answers that 2PM would be fine, the prior suggestion carries.

SECOND MEETING

If a client and a salesperson need to make another meeting, begin the next meeting by reviewing what happened in your last meeting.

Salesperson:	"The last time we talked, you indicated that you wanted to purchase some large paintings to enhance your new corporate office space. You also indicated that you would be interested in any discount we could offer you if you were to purchase a body of work all at one time; isn't that right?"
Client:	"Yes, that's right, but today our main focus is to get a large painting for the reception area."
Salesperson:	"So you are saying that today you are interested in finding one painting to enhance your reception area, is that right?"
Client:	"Yes, that's right. We have decided that it is important to act immediately and decorate our reception area. Then, at a later time, we can talk more about the rest of the office."
Salesperson:	"Very well then, let's pick out just the right painting for that space. I'm assuming that if we can find something today that you like for that space, you will want to go ahead with it. Is that right?

This last statement is an example of a test close. If the client says yes, then all you need to do is find the perfect solution to the client's problem.

OFFERING DISCOUNTS

One thing you could do in a situation like this, to keep your client working with you, is to offer a discount on the painting that the client is purchasing today, if the client continues to use you to help find just the right artwork for the rest of the office at a later time. Let the client know that if more artwork is purchased from you in the future, you will be able to give a discount on those future works as well as on this purchase.

TIE-DOWNS

Listening carefully and asking specific questions will help you build confidence and rapport. We can call this "friendly selling" or "relationship selling" or "gentle selling." Asking questions and listening is the one thing that will always build trust and rapport. If you don't remember anything else about selling art, remember that.

One effective way of questioning is to use minor reflexive questions. Get in the habit of using them in your everyday conversations. Then they will slip out naturally during your sales meetings. Some sales trainers call minor reflexive questions "tie-downs," because when used at the end of a sentence, they will demand a "yes" answer or they will "raise an objection."

MINOR REFLEXIVE QUESTIONS

Can't you?	Didn't you?	Isn't it?
Wasn't it?	Aren't you?	Don't you agree?
Doesn't it?	Wouldn't it?	Shouldn't it?
Haven't you?	Didn't it?	Won't you?

When you make a statement, simply add the appropriate question at the end of a sentence to get agreement. If you don't hear the client say anything, it doesn't mean that the question wasn't heard. I have found that in most cases the agreement is so automatic and understood that the person will not feel it is even necessary to respond. If the client really doesn't agree, you will hear about it.

EXERCISE

Read the following statements and cover the tie-downs in the right column with a piece of paper. See if you can easily add the tie-down to each statement before you look at them.

STATEMENT	TIE-DOWN
These prints are unique,	aren't they?
Permanence is important,	isn't it?
You would like to have a beautiful collection of original art someday,	wouldn't you?

Concentration is the secret of strength in politics, in war, in trade, in short in all management of human affairs.
Ralph Waldo Emerson

She has really chosen the right colors to fit with her living room decor,	hasn't she?
This sculpture is captivating from any point of view,	isn't it?
You can look at this as a nice addition to your print collection,	can't you?
We do want the work properly framed to insure the safety of the piece,	don't we?
With the right frame, this work will fit into any collection,	don't you agree?
She has created a beautiful balance of color and composition,	hasn't she?

Tie-downs are easy to learn, aren't they? You are learning them right now, aren't you? It's amazing how they seem to just slip out naturally, don't they? You should practice them, though, shouldn't you? They can easily become a speech habit, can't they? When you use a tie-down, it is important to wait for the client's answer, isn't it?

EXERCISE II

Practice talking to a friend about art (or the art that you sell), using tie-downs. Continue until they feel natural. I encourage you to practice tie-downs during short conversations you have over the next few days until you get good at using them.

Listening builds trust; talking alone doesn't.

EXERCISE III

Now practice tie-downs by putting them at the beginning of a sentence.

It's a very distinctive piece, isn't it? Will change to…

Isn't it distinctive?

It is a fascinating piece, isn't it? Will change to…

Isn't it fascinating?

It would go well in your living room, wouldn't it? Will change to…

Wouldn't it go well in your living room?

She has created a beautiful balance of color and composition, hasn't she? Will change to…

Hasn't she created a beautiful balance of color and composition?

LISTENING SKILLS

People enjoy being recognized and acknowledged. Art can add recognition, identity, beauty, enjoyment, memories, good feelings, as well as pride of ownership to people's lives.

If you ask questions about your clients' feelings in relation to an art piece, and then listen intently, you will validate and acknowledge them. It is a high form of communication. By simply asking for feedback—how they see, feel and experience the work—you will encourage them to speak of their appreciation of the work. They will not be able to share their personal feelings about a work unless they really experience it, so they will have to see and study before they can tell you what they think. When they do, we must realize that they are not so much judging the work as expressing personal feelings about it. Always listen with an open and accepting mind. The way people see or hear is based on their own unique experience. Give them an opportunity and plenty of time to get involved in the experience of an artwork. Acknowledge your clients for their unique viewpoint and taste. This is really a creative process for you and for the art buyer. After they have experienced a work, they will be more ready to own it.

BECOMING A GOOD LISTENER

The best way to become a good listener is to *not talk*. I remember a time when I was shopping for a new car. The salesman just listened to me. Didn't say much, didn't ask much. I remember thinking to myself, this car salesman is really different. When he did say something, I trusted what he said. I felt he knew and he cared.

There is no faster way to build trust than by listening. There is no faster way to undermine trust and annoy a person than by talking too much. When you listen intently to a person, it shows that you genuinely care, and that person's self-esteem goes up. The person feels more worthwhile and important as a human being. When it shows that you are happy to be listening, you can create a real bond of trust and affection. The more trust and affection a person feels toward you, the easier it will be for her to be in agreement with you.

By listening in a genuine, caring way to everything a client has to say, you can make the person feel terrific. Begin practicing every day in every area of your life, not just when you are selling.

It is very important that you become a good listener.

91

DON'T INTERRUPT

We listen to what we value, and we ignore what we don't value. The fastest way to turn a person against you, or hurt her feelings, is to ignore what she is saying. Even worse is to interrupt the person in the middle of a sentence or thought; it's like an emotional slap in the face. When this happens, the process of building trust or affection is likely to be terminated.

GUIDELINES TO BECOMING A GOOD LISTENER

➤ Listen intently to every word the person is saying.

➤ Look at the person. Give him steady and warm eye contact. Don't be shy, but don't stare him down.

➤ Be genuinely interested in what she is saying.

➤ Listen with the intention to assist the person best to meet his needs or desires.

➤ Ask only appropriate questions to gain the information necessary for you to respond or act in a meaningful way. Listen carefully to the answers.

➤ Let the person know that you are listening by paraphrasing what he just said to you.

➤ Take notes when appropriate so that you can refer to the information later. When a person sees you doing this, she will know that you are listening carefully and that you want to remember what is being said. You might want to explain to them why you are taking notes.

➤ Resolve to become a good listener. Practice on every occasion you can, be it a sales situation or everyday conversation.

➤ Seek out opportunities to make others feel important by listening attentively to what they say.

➤ Remember that you have two ears and one mouth. Learn to listen twice as much as you talk.

THE POWER OF THE PAUSE

One of the best listening skills is to simply pause before replying. When your client finishes saying something, rather than jumping in immediately with the first thing you can think of, take a moment (two or three seconds), and pause quietly before you answer. Remember, being a good listener builds trust.

THE BENEFITS OF PAUSING

➤ You avoid the risk of interrupting if your client is just gathering her thoughts.

➤ If you don't answer right away, your client may continue speaking and give you more information to help you meet the person's needs and make the sale.

➤ Putting some silence into a conversation compliments the person. Your client will know you are carefully considering what is being said. You are silently saying that what is being said is important to you and worthy of quiet reflection. You make the person feel more valuable and this raises his feelings of self-esteem.

➤ It appears you are letting the statement or question soak into your mind.

➤ With some time to consider what was said, you won't be immediately looking for something or anything to say. You will be better prepared to consider the situation and make the appropriate response.

➤ Pausing will show that you are an exceptional conversationalist.

APPLYING LISTENING SKILLS TO ART SALES

There is no faster way to irritate a potential client than by talking too much and listening too little. According to the Purchasing Manager's Association of America's annual survey, the biggest single irritant that potential buyers experience in dealing with salespeople is, "They talk too much."

Salespeople typically like to talk. Sometimes it is out of nervousness; sometimes it is to avoid selling. When working with a potential buyer, it is important to listen—not just listen so that you can respond. Listen carefully to find out the client's needs and

Perhaps there is only one cardinal sin: impatience. Because of impatience we are driven out of Paradise; because of impatience we cannot return.
Franz Kafka

The most successful sales people know how to ask questions and then listen.

desires. What does the client really want?

A good practice is to try to answer questions and then make an inquiry. Pause. Wait for an answer. Allow the client to have a chance to think. Don't rush the client. Don't talk so fast that the client will have to speed up just to be able to say something.

Match the pace of your client. If your client talks slowly and deliberately, adopt to the same pace. If your client talks fast, then speed up to match it. You can always add pauses if the pace becomes too fast for you. Never say more than three sentences in a row without pausing.

COUNT TO THREE

When your client stops talking, pause before responding. Get into the habit of counting to three. A count-of-three-pause gives you a chance to absorb what has been said. It shows the client that you are listening and you value her words and thoughts.

➤ It shows that what has been said is worthy of consideration.

➤ It helps ensure that you will not interrupt the client.

➤ It gives you a chance to think of the most appropriate response.

It is imperative that you say something after you pause. A pause without a reply is very rude. The silent treatment will destroy any rapport you have established. Some people use silence as a means of controlling a situation where two people are not in agreement, but it will only cause discomfort or resentment in the other person.

➤ Never sound sarcastic, cynical, argumentative, or in any way angry.

➤ Never cut a person off or try to change the subject.

➤ Never look uninterested or bored.

➤ Don't try to sound or look "cool."

➤ Be calm and sincere.

Try to respond honestly and in agreement as much as possible. Help the client see that you are there to understand and assist. Before responding with your point of view, ask at least one clarifying question. This will give the client a chance to rephrase or reevaluate her thoughts.

Tell the client what you think you heard in your own words:

> "Let me see if I've got it right. What you are saying is …"

Or, you might say:

> "If I understand you correctly …" and then repeat or rephrase what you think the client said.

Both of these responses demonstrate that you have been attentive. They show that you are making an effort to understand, and that you are genuinely interested in the client's thoughts and feelings. Look directly and gently at the client while he or she is talking. Don't stare. Smile. Be receptive and polite.

By becoming a good listener, you become good company. People will want to be around you. Clients will feel welcome and relaxed when they are with you. Remember that listening to a person builds trust and affection between the two of you. The more you practice listening skills, the more your client will appreciate your opinions and consider your recommendations.

As you practice these skills, you will gain self-discipline and confidence when you communicate with your clients. It is said that our minds can process 500 to 600 words a minute but we can only speak about 150 words a minute. It takes real effort to stay focused on what a person is saying. If you are not disciplined in conversation, your mind will wander in a hundred different directions. Ask for clarification. Your client will respect you for it.

EXERCISE

Pair up with a friend and carry on a conversation about art. Pause for a few seconds before you respond to each question or statement. Do this until it feels natural. Practice pausing in your conversations during the next few days until you get used to it. It may feel strange at first, especially if you are a person who is used to talking fast and has a proclivity to be impatient. If I just described you, this is the very kind of practice you need. Try it and watch your relationships improve.

Stay focused and listen carefully to what your client has to say.

95

STORIES SELL

Most artists and their works have some kind of story. Some actually depict a story—a biblical story, a historical story, a personal story, for example. There is a story behind the way or reason the painting, sculpture or print came to be made. There is a personal story behind the artist's commitment to make the work. All of these stories will add a high degree of interest to the work. If you know the story, tell it. Only tell the story to a client who wants to hear it, though.

Client: "I don't understand what this is about."

Salesperson: "There is a story here. Would you like to hear it?"

Client: "Why, yes."

Salesperson: "Would you like the long version or the short version?"

Client: "I've got time. Give me the full story."

Now you have permission to relate the story. If you find that the client is starting to lose interest, finish up the story quickly. At the end of the story, you might say:

Salesperson: "Now that you know the story, the painting makes a lot more sense, doesn't it?"

As a salesperson, try to find out the stories behind the work you represent. Make good notes so that you can tell the stories well.

If you are the artist, you already know the stories. Think what might be of interest to a prospective buyer. Then, with the client's permission, tell the stories.

PUT THE STORIES IN WRITING

A few years ago, I exhibited 60 watercolor paintings in a one-man show. There was so much work that I was concerned that people would get into the exhibition space and feel overwhelmed. Guests might not take the time to really look at the work. So I wrote a short story about each work and mounted it on the wall next to each piece. When people came to the show, they took their time looking at the paintings and reading the stories. It took some time to write and mount the stories, but it was well wroth the effort. I'm sure that the stories helped sell paintings.

WRITING IT DOWN

One of the best ways you can demonstrate to your clients that you care and that you are listening is to take notes while they are talking. If a client objects for some reason, simply tell the person that you always do this so that you won't forget something important. Tell the person that it helps you listen carefully and remember what is being said.

The first time I wrote during a sale was with a corporate client. The buyer came to my studio and began looking at works. When he found something that he liked, I wrote down the title of the piece and its price. I knew that there was a budget and I had an idea of what the budget was. As he was looking, more and more titles were added. He selected paintings, original prints, and even a poster. I couldn't believe that he would buy all of the works that he liked. I expected that we would go through the list and eliminate some. I was sure that if he selected all of the pieces he liked, it would be over his budget. But of course I didn't say that. He saw that I was writing notes. After going through many works and selecting quite a number, he said to me, "Let's see what I've got." He asked me to add up all the prices and give him a total. To my great surprise, when I closed the sale, he took them all! That is exactly why you take notes.

Write down particular facts that the client gives you. Write down the client's likes and dislikes. Your writing also will help you pause during the conversation. You can use your writing time as a pause and then follow up with a question. Writing also helps you be less intrusive in your client's space. Your client will have a chance to look more deeply at the artworks while you occupy yourself with writing. There are other benefits too:

➤ You will remember what the person told you.

➤ Writing makes the words communicated more "solid," more important.

➤ It will help you to not forget anything important.

➤ You will be able to keep an account of what they like.

➤ You will be able to make an easy transition to writing up the order.

➤ You will be able to review your notes later to prepare for a future appointment with the client.

➤ You will be able to apply what you learn to other clients and other situations.

➤ You will have a record to refer back to at any time.

➤ You will be able to review with your client what has been said and agreed upon.

In some situations, writing may not be appropriate or even possible. But if you can do it and you can make it feel comfortable and natural, it will help increase your sales.

❑ Selling is a question-and-answer process.

❑ When your client answers your questions thoughtfully, it means she is interested in buying.

❑ Qualify as soon as you can.

❑ The most successful salespeople know how to ask questions and then to listen.

❑ If you listen very carefully to what your client asks and says, you will discover his prime factor.

❑ If you focus on the client's prime factor, you will build rapport and ultimately make the sale.

❑ When you meet a client for a second time, always review what you discussed or decided at the end of your first meeting before beginning the second meeting.

❑ When clients know that you are listening and that you care about their needs, you build trust.

❑ Never tell your clients that you know just what they will like. You don't!

❑ Always ask questions your client can answer.

❑ Use tie-downs at the end of sentences to get agreement or raise objections. Practice them until they slip out naturally.

❑ Give your clients an opportunity and plenty of time to personally experience a work of art.

❑ Validate and acknowledge your clients for their unique viewpoint and taste.

❑ Listening will help your client feel more confident when making a buying decision.

CHAPTER SUMMARY

❑ Paraphrase the important things your client says.

❑ As a salesperson, know the stories behind a work.

❑ With the client's permission, tell the stories that you think will be of interest about the works you are selling.

❑ Always end your story with a question.

❑ Post interesting information next to a painting at an exhibit.

❑ Get in the habit of pausing for a few seconds during all your conversations.

❑ Never interrupt a client who is talking to you. Wait to be sure she is finished.

❑ Plan always to have your "notebook" handy when working with a serious buyer.

❑ Start writing from the beginning of the meeting.

❑ If you write during the meeting it will be an easy transition to writing up the order.

❑ Go back and review your notes to help you remember and learn.

SOME TO
CHOICE
CLIENTS TO THE

Chapter 8
Connectors

18 ways to connect clients to the art

Handling rejection

Either you are a creature of circumstance or the creator of circumstance.
Robert Cavett

18 WAYS TO CONNECT CLIENTS TO THE ART

Help your clients establish a strong personal connection with the artwork that attracts them. Some of these connections are rational; most are emotional. Use them as bridges. Try to find out what the strongest connection is between your client and the artwork that he is admiring. Go with that. Then add others if you feel it necessary.

Whatever a person thinks about a piece, it is their opinion—it is not right or wrong. It doesn't matter how **you** feel when you are closing a sale. Train yourself to connect a person to the piece emotionally or rationally by asking questions. Always satisfy questions about technique, the artist, the medium, the size, etc., and then move to connect the buyer with her feelings by asking another question. People buy art for emotional reasons. You could say,

> "See how the artist uses the medium to bring you into the image (story, situation). Can you feel the emotion, the spirit, the passion here?"

Of course, these questions and the ones that follow are only given as suggestions. Use your own creativity to know just what to say that will be appropriate in each situation. Put these ideas into your own words; don't try to memorize the examples. The other thing to remember is the ABC's of closing—<u>a</u>lways <u>b</u>e <u>c</u>losing!

1. OPINIONS

Buyers have their own opinions. They don't know how you feel and there is no need to tell them unless they ask you. Many clients don't care how you feel. Most people have very strong opinions about art, what they like, and what they don't like. Don't try to change them. If you happen to agree with their opinion, expressing your agreement will help strengthen their opinion. Often, people feel deeply but will not trust their feelings because they may not know a lot about art or the particular art they are seeing. You can help validate their feelings by reassuring them that they are relevant. If they ask you how you feel, tell them—but only if they ask. There is no need to volunteer this information, especially if it is not about a favorite painting or artist of yours. What appeals to you will not necessarily appeal to someone else.

When you are dealing with a couple, they need to be able to talk alone. Give them a safe space to do that. Either leave them with the piece and walk out of earshot, or leave them alone in the viewing room. Before you exit, however, review with them what they mutually like.

2. OPTIONS

Here are some questions you may wish to use to find out what your clients' options are:

> "How can you see it being used?"

> "Where do you see this hanging?"

> "Where will you display it?"

> "Who will see it?"

> "How will it be appreciated?"

> "If you were to own this piece, how would it harmonize or contrast with the other art you own?"

> "What possibilities (or alternatives) do you have?"

> "Can you visualize this in your home or office?"

This last question is a strong suggestion to your client to actually picture the place where it will be installed. When you ask this question, be sure to wait for the answer. If he answers yes, that is a successful test close.

3. UNDERSTANDING

Clients may not be aware of the artist or the work. If you are the artist, you are the best source to enlighten them. First, politely find out if they are interested in learning more about the work or the artist. Second, only offer as much info as they really want to know. Sometimes, when clients learn more about how a work was made or what it means, they will be more interested in owning the work. Here are some more questions you might ask:

> "Are you familiar with this artist's work?"

"Would you like to hear some facts about the work?"

"Would you like to know how this piece was made?"

"Do you know how this artist was trained? It is quite an interesting story."

4. LEARNING

Many art students, young and old, buy art because it inspires them or will teach them how to make their own work better. They will buy it so that they can study the technique or the way it was made.

We can also learn about ourselves from a work of art. An art piece can inspire us to look deeper into ourselves, to live more fulfilling lives.

It doesn't hurt to know something about art history. If you know your art history, you can offer information that will make the piece relevant in a historical context.

"What do you think we can learn from this work?"

"Can you see the influence of the (name the art history period such as the impressionists, the realists, pop art, Baroque art, Renaissance art, etc.) in this work?"

5. REMINDING

This is probably one of the most powerful connectors. It is also one of the easiest to speak about with a client.

"What does this piece remind you of?

"What sport, person, landscape, travel experience, event, place, hobby, occupation, book, movie, musical composition, play, opera, family event does this piece remind you of?"

Memory is a very powerful reason for people to buy art. A portrait of Johnny when he was 10, Dad when he retired, Mom when she was president of the Floral Society—all are reminders. A portrait of the family pet, the horse, or the boat will hang as a proud and sentimental reminder of the good times. The painting of a beach in Hawaii will remind the family of their vacation. The painting of a waterfall in Yosemite Valley will remind the family of the awesome inspiration they felt when they visited this popular national park. People love to buy art that reminds them of a person, a passion, a positive experience. Here are some more sample questions:

"Doesn't this remind you of your travels to _____?"

"Wouldn't this be a perfect reminder of your holiday?"

"Doesn't this remind you of some of the finest craftsmanship in the world?"

"Doesn't this remind you of [name another great work of art]?"

"Do you play (name a sport, musical instrument, or game)?"

"Have you ever visited Venice, Italy? spent time in Paris? been to the Louvre Museum?"

"Have you seen the film about _____ or read the story of _____?"

6. SEEING

A person can see a metaphor in a butterfly, a phoenix, a tower, a sunset, a sunrise, a flower, etc. For example, a person might see the lightness of being in a bronze sculpture of a dancer. Of course the visual arts are all about seeing. Seeing can take place on many levels. Here are some sample questions to give you ideas:

"What do you see in the work?

"What colors … images … forms … textures … compositions … melodies … rhythms do you see?"

"Do you see the beauty…the simplicity…the craftsmanship … the delicate care of the artist?

"Do you see the drama … the perfection?"

"Do you see the humor?"

"Do you see the metaphor?"

"Do you see the [name the color]?"

7. ENTHUSIASM

When people are "hit" by an image, they will most likely voice some kind of exclamation. As the seller, you will be ready to notice the sounds, words, or movements that they make. It will be a sure signal to you that they are interested in the work. If you also feel that enthusiasm for the piece, it will help you bond with them and move toward the state of "being in agreement."

8. FEELING

There are many connections —all reasons for people to trade money for artworks. Be aware of these connections, and use the ones that apply to the work you are selling.

A client might sense the emotional concerns or values of the artist or feel a deep emotional connection with the imagery. An artwork can stir up the emotions of its viewer. Go to an art museum sometime, sit quietly in a gallery and listen to the comments people make to each other as they view the works of art. Take notes.

"How does it make you feel?"

"How do you feel when you experience this piece?"

"What other relevant experiences have you had?"

"It sure beats a blank wall, doesn't it?"

"Can you feel the drama?"

"Can you feel the space?"

"How does the color feel?"

9. EMPATHY

Your client might have sympathy with the emotional or political position of the artist. What was the artist feeling? The artist's personal vision of the world is revealed in the piece, and your client relates to it. The artist may have a personal mission to educate the public on some social or political issue. Your client may feel empathy for the artist's view. This is a strong connector.

10. LIKE OR DISLIKE

Find out what your client likes and dislikes. People buy what they like. They don't buy what they don't like. It is that simple.

Never be afraid to find out what people don't like. You need to know. Every so often, when you find out that people don't like something about a work, it is because they don't understand it. On occasion, when you explain a work of art, it will change their perception. Often, dislike is a result of either lack of knowledge or misunderstanding. If a particular client frowns or mentions something that she doesn't like, ask her about it. Sometimes, when she talks about it, a new understanding will come to light and her negative opinion will be turned around. It is better for your clients to have their own insight than it is for you to try to explain to them. Rather than explain, ask questions that will lead them to a more clear understanding. It will make them feel validated and in control if they make their own discoveries.

11. HUMAN CONNECTIONS

How do we relate as a member of the human race? Any time a figurative image is used in an artwork, there is a connection to its viewers. Look at art through the ages. Walk through the Louvre in Paris or the Metropolitan Museum of Art in New York City. Notice the many references to human imagery. It is a subject that has been used since time immemorial and will continue to be used in art.

> "Look at that lightness of being in the dancer's form."

> "What a powerful stance!"

> "What a gesture of defiance!"

> "Look at the human dignity and strength in that image."

"Can you see how the strength of the figure is enhanced by the size and mass of the sculptural form?"

"Notice how the artist has captured a vivid moment of great feeling and spiritual passion through the physical form."

12. GOVERNMENT AND POLITICAL CONNECTIONS

Governmental bodies will commission works for government buildings and landscaped gardens. Political leaders will commission portraits. This avenue alone can be a source of repeat sales once you are established as an artist or a dealer.

13. EXCITING

People can get very excited about an art piece. Many will openly express that excitement. Here are some sample questions:

"What is it that grabs your attention?"

"What excites you most about this work?"

"Why do you think it excites you so much?"

"I can see your excitement; what is it that grabs you?"

The image could be an exciting battle, a sporting event, a fight, a celebration. The human body can be exciting. Animals can be exciting. Colors can be exciting. Compositions can be exciting.

14. PASSION

Help your client experience the passion of the artist, the artist's conviction. When an artist feels deeply about a cause or issue and puts that out to the world through artwork, it can result in powerful work.

"You can sense the strong passion this artist feels toward his people."

"Do you share the passion this artist feels for the hungry?"

"Can you feel the tender passion she has for war victims?"

15. RELIGIOUS CONNECTIONS

Each religion has specific art traditions. When you know that clients have strong religious beliefs, this can be the reason why they want to own a work that relates to that religion or reminds them of their affiliations. Examples: Baptist, Buddhist, Christian, Confucian, Episcopalian, Greek Orthodox, Hindu, Islamic, Jewish, Lutheran, Methodist, Protestant, Roman Catholic, Zen Buddhist.

Art has been used in places of worship for many centuries. Religious institutions are an important market for the world of art. Often, artworks are commissioned by a religious institution. An artist will be hired to make a "cartoon" for a larger piece; the commission will be granted when the preliminary study is approved.

If you represent an artist who does this kind of work, you will sell the idea with the preliminary cartoon. Usually an artist is given an advance partial payment and then full payment when the commission is completed and delivered.

16. ETHNIC CONNECTIONS

Look for ethnic connections, cultural identities, national loyalties, racial connections. People like to be able to identify with their own ethnic, national or cultural roots.

17. SENSUAL CONNECTIONS

Connect your clients to art through their senses—hearing, touch, sight, taste, smell; seeing the sound of the ocean, hearing a symphony of light, tasting the colors, smelling the passion, feeling the texture, touching the heart. Be creative; ask questions that will open up their senses.

18. SPIRITUAL CONNECTIONS

Here is a beautiful and powerful message: When an artist is communicating her personal experience of the universe, God, the supreme power, spiritual energy, the light of life, the soul, the life force, human spirituality, the result can be very moving work. Art of this nature can be a great source of personal inspiration when displayed in a home or a public place. Look at the many works of art that have been created through the ages depicting political and religious stories.

HANDLING REJECTION

If someone doesn't buy from you, that doesn't mean that you are being rejected. It simply means that he chose not to take advantage of the opportunity you offered.

It may be true that if you had used different words, or conducted yourself in a different way, you could have made the sale. More likely, however, no matter what you said, he would not have bought anything.

Fear of failure can discourage you from taking action—not selling is not failing, it is simply not selling. You have lost nothing. When you do sell, everyone wins. Your clients take possession of the art they love and you are rewarded with the money you want or need.

APMA

Never go into a selling situation expecting to be rejected. Remember to keep an APMA—anything's possible mental attitude. No matter how many clients have walked away, that doesn't mean your next client will do the same. Look at your batting average. If you sell to one in ten, then each client who doesn't buy will be just one of the nine you must approach to get the sale.

Remember, you don't want to sell to people who don't want the art you represent. Help people own what they really want. Not everyone will want what you are selling.

Look at your selling efforts as an adventure. As you practice selling, you will become more comfortable with the process.

CHAPTER SUMMARY

❏ Use questions to help clients see and feel connections to the art they are viewing.

❏ Questions empower you in a sales conversation. It is with questions that you find out a person's qualifications, needs, considerations, and objections.

❏ Do your homework so that you know what questions to ask.

❏ Learn as much as you can about the art and the artist.

❏ Ask questions that will enhance your clients' enjoyment and knowledge of the works and the artists who created them.

❏ Keep an APMA—anything's possible mental attitude.

❏ Only help people own what they really want.

Chapter 9
Closing

Test closing

Closing a sale

The puppy dog close

What selling art requires

Never continue a job you don't enjoy. If you're happy in what you are doing, you'll like yourself, you'll have inner peace. And if you have that along with physical health, you will have had more success than you could possibly have imagine. Johnny Carson

TEST CLOSING

A test close is a question that tests the client's involvement in the artwork to see if she is ready to make the commitment to own it. There are many ways to test-close the sale.

CONDITIONAL QUESTION

A conditional question works very well. If . . . then . . . ?

> "If you were to own this piece, where would you want to hang it?"

ALTERNATIVE CHOICE

Another great way to test-close is to use an alternate or choice question.

> "If you were to own this piece, would it be for your office or your home?"

Here are some examples of test closes. You can begin using them to assess your clients interest before you try to close the sale:

> "If you were to get this painting, would you want to keep it in this frame or would you want to have it framed yourself?"

> "Can you visualize this hanging in your living room?"

> "This would be a great reminder of your wonderful vacation here, don't you agree?'

> "Are you seriously considering owning this print?"

> "I would be delighted to see you take this home; I can see you really love it, don't you?"

> "Would you be taking it with you, or would you want me to ship it to you?"

> "If you had plenty of money, would you take advantage of this offer?"

Ask and you get; don't ask and you don't get.
Hank Trisler

The closing question is the question that asks the client in a very direct way to own or invest in the work(s) of art being admired. It is amazing how many people who want to sell art don't ask their clients to buy. If you don't ask your clients to buy, they probably won't. It is your loss, but, more importantly, it is their loss.

A closing question usually must be asked for a sale to take place. The answer to a closing question will either seal the agreement or raise an objection. If an objection comes up, you take care of the issue and close again. Once in a while, a person will come up to you with checkbook in hand and ask you to figure the tax. That is rare and most likely will happen when the art is priced under $500.

ASKING THE QUESTIONS

Therefore, you must learn to ask the closing question in a natural and easy way. Ask it with a smile and when rapport is very high. Ask a closing question when you recognize that your client is interested in owning the artwork(s) and may be ready to make that commitment. Here are some friendly closes. They are short, simple to learn and easy to use. If you don't memorize anything else from this book, learn a few of these. Practice them with a friend until you are comfortable saying them. Let them innocently, freely and gently slip out of your mouth at the appropriate time.

12 EASY-TO-LEARN CLOSES

➤ Would you like it (them)?

➤ Do you want it (them)?

➤ Is it yours? Are they yours?

➤ Are you going to take it?

➤ Are you taking it with you?

➤ Well, if you like it, why don't you take it?

➤ Can you take it (a challenge)?

➤ Is that it?

➤ Shall we go ahead?

CLOSING A SALE

If you don't ask the client to buy, she probably won't buy.

➤ Is that the one you want? (to get)?

➤ Shall we do the paperwork?

➤ Did you want to use a credit card or a personal check?

TONE OF VOICE

Just as important as the words you use is the tone of voice in which they are delivered. Speak with honesty and sincerity in your voice. Be gentle and kind when you are asking for the sale.

SILENCE IS GOLDEN

When you ask a test close or a closing question, it is imperative that you wait silently for a reply. A test-closing question will tell you whether a person is ready to make a decision. A closing question will ask your client to make a decision to buy or not to buy. When you ask one of these questions, it is very important to pause until your client answers. Sometimes it may take your client a good amount of time to reply. They will want to consider their answer carefully. You, as the artist or salesperson, must remain silent until the answer comes, no matter what—even if it takes them five, 10, or 15 minutes. Usually the answer will come in the first 10 seconds, but not always. Even 10 seconds can seem like a long time. You are anxious to hear the answer. They are not anxious to spend their money. They may want to own the art very much, and you know that, but the money can get in the way. They may not be sure they are getting the best price. They may not be sure they want to own that piece. They may not be sure they want to spend the money for this. There can be all sorts of uncertainties that come into their making that decision. You must wait for them to answer. Don't let yourself break the silence. Remember, it is their turn to answer the question. Just stay quiet and wait for their answer.

If anything is worth trying at all, it's worth trying at least ten times.
Art Linkletter

EXERCISE

Pair up with a friend and ask each other closing questions. Smile warmly and ask with genuine interest. The person acting as the buyer must wait at least 10 seconds before giving an answer. The one acting as the salesperson must always wait silently for the partner to answer. Be aware of what is going on while waiting for an answer. Do you feel tension in your body? Fear of rejection? Apprehension? Anticipation? What thoughts are you having? Even though you are play-acting, the real emotions that you would experience in the situation will be there. The mind does not know the difference between fact and fiction. Your mind and body are conditioned to react. Look at your partner's face with great interest when asking these questions. After you do the exercise, report what you saw expressed on the other's face. Become aware of your own feelings and report these to your partner. With practice, you will find that self-awareness can override feelings of fear or anxiety. Repeat the exercise with the roles switched. Remember that awareness is the key.

KEEP A NEUTRAL POSITION

If you have some anxiety, it will be communicated. Detach yourself from the outcome. Just stay neutral and wait for the answer. Be willing to accept a yes, a maybe, or a no. Sometimes that is difficult in a real situation when there are thousands of dollars resting on the client's decision. You will have a better chance of succeeding if you keep a neutral stance. Whatever the client says, it is okay. Even if the client tries to avoid answering by saying that he wants to think it over or needs to talk it over, or is not sure, stay neutral and accept his answer. Then you will be able to respond appropriately.

TECHNIQUES TO REMAIN CALM AND COMFORTABLE WHILE CLOSING

➤ Examine with interest the other person's face and the artwork. Think of it as a threesome—the client, you, and the artwork. You can move your attention from your client to the work and back to your client while he is making up his mind about what to say.

➤ Counting silently while waiting may also help keep you neutral. Make it a game and see how many seconds it takes the client to answer your question.

➤ Breathing while selling will help you stay relaxed. Being aware of your breathing when you ask the closing question will help you

Some people say that it is helpful to synchronize your breathing to that of your client.

remain neutral. Put your attention on the breaths you are taking. Some people say that it is helpful to synchronize your breathing to that of your client as a way of increasing rapport. It is reported to be a very subtle and effective way to establish a strong communication with another person. Take a moment here and just breathe and be aware of your breath. Feel the calm that aware breathing can produce in your being. This can also help you establish the peaceful atmosphere needed for optimal closing.

THE QUESTION

Closing is the most important part of the selling process. Most sales take place because the representative asks a closing question. Don't expect your client to buy without hearing a closing question. It can happen, but it is rare.

The important thing is to make a safe, relaxed space in which your clients can make a decision. Become aware of your hidden feelings—your fears and anxiety. If a "giving-up" impulse comes, let it go. Do not give it power or feed it by fearing it.

There may also be cultural differences when asking closing questions, such as position of bodies to each other, eye contact, etc.

➤ Keep your hands out of your pockets and at your sides. Hands in the pockets present an image of apology or inferiority. A pocketed hand can also communicate subliminally that you have something to hide. You may think it looks cool, but it doesn't communicate that message in a selling situation.

➤ Don't hold your hands in front of you or behind your back.

➤ Don't fold your arms. Folded arms communicate superiority. You want to remain neutral.

Ask the closing question when the time is right. Like water boiling in the pot on the stove, it is as hot as it is going to get. As soon as you remove the pot, it will begin to cool. If you leave it off the stove for a day, it will be as cold as if it were never heated up at all. If you don't ask the question when you know the client is ready, the person is likely to forget why he or she was so eager to make the purchase in the first place. You will lose the sale and the client will lose the opportunity to have and enjoy that work of art for years to come.

A WEAK CLOSING QUESTION

An example of a weak close is, "Well, what do you think?" This does not ask the person to make a buying decision. The answer to this question will probably not be a yes answer or an objection. It will side-track your closing attempt. Never ask this question!

DEFINITION OF A CLOSE

A close is a question asked to assist the client in making a decision from which the client will benefit.

Remember, you are interested in gaining clients and collectors more than art sales. We are not trying to con anyone into buying art. A con man will sell anything to anybody. He doesn't care what happens after the sale. Professional artists or art representatives will only sell what they truly believe will benefit their clients.

WHEN TO CLOSE

➤ When the pace feels relaxed

➤ When the client shows great interest

➤ When the client begins to ask questions

WHERE TO CLOSE

Anywhere	At the golf course
In the parking lot	In the gallery
In the home	At their office
At an art fair	In your studio

ALWAYS BE CLOSING

The ABC's of closing are always be closing, which means that each step of the selling process is a step toward closing the sale. Look at it as if you were going down a stairway with your client. You will know you have reached the bottom of the stairway when you ask a closing question and the buyer says yes and owns the work of art. I like the analogy of going down a stairway better than climbing stairs. Climbing implies effort. Let the whole process be comfortable, gentle and as effortless as possible. When you can make the experience of selling art fun and effortless, you will be very successful.

Don't assist a person in making a decision that he or she will later regret.

119

THE PUPPY-DOG CLOSE

Have a client take an artwork home, and inevitably he will buy it.

The puppy-dog close is based on the idea that if you take a puppy home for a few days, you will end up falling in love with it and buy it. This is a great way to sell art as well. Many galleries will let you take a piece home for a week or two with the idea that you will want to keep it after that time. The best way to introduce this close is to offer a hesitant client the opportunity to live with the art for a few days, with no strings attached. If the client agrees to try it, at the end of the trial period he or she most likely will buy the work.

You need to ensure that the client will not run away with the art by "swiping" her credit card for the full amount of the sale. At the end of the trial period, if the client brings it back, you will credit the full amount back to the account. If the client keeps the work, you have already been paid.

I have also managed to sell quite a bit of art using the puppy-dog close with friends. On occasion I have let good friends borrow multiple works unsecured for a period of months. Their homeowners' or businessowners' insurance covered the works while they were in their possession. They have ended up buying 75% of the works.

As an artist, I can always use more storage space. Occasionally, friends have blank walls in their new homes or offices. They ask me if I would like to hang some paintings on their walls. I always know that this is a great opportunity to sell art if I know the people well. They initially think that they will just be borrowing the art, but invariably they want to keep it.

RENTING OR LEASING ART

Another way to use the puppy-dog close is to rent or lease artwork to prospective clients. Many corporate offices like to rent rather than buy. Some will rent while they are considering buying. This can be a way of increasing your month-to-month income while the client falls in love with the work. In any rental situation, discuss the possibility of an eventual purchase. You can explain and negotiate your terms. Artists and rental galleries can offer to deduct a portion of the rent paid from the selling price if the client decides to buy after having rented a work of art for a period of time (usually not more than a year).

Art leases to offices can also turn into residential sales. People who work in an office often want to take the art home. This kind of business works well when you are selling original prints, serigraphs, lithographs, etchings, woodcuts, or sculpture castings, where there are multiples available.

Be sure that all lease or month-to-month rental agreements are in writing. Make sure that the works are insured while they are in the possession of the lessee. Either you or the client will be liable for damage or theft of the art. The insurance fees can be part of the lease or they can be included in the homeowners' or businessowners' insurance policy. All of these factors must be discussed and agreed upon in writing.

PAYMENT PLANS

Since art is a luxury item and can be expensive, many buyers may not have the cash ready to spend. Most galleries have payment programs to help customers finance their purchases. These programs can vary greatly and are usually tailored to the individual collector. Since paying off credit card debt can be very expensive, a gallery can make a sale more attractive to a client by offering terms with low interest or even no interest over a short period of time, usually limited to one year.

If a person is not paying for the piece all at once, it is important for the artist or gallery to retain possession of the work until the piece is paid for in full. This avoids the complications of trying to take back a work that has not been completely paid for or trying to get overdue payments for a work that the client has already obtained. This is true no matter who the client is. With rare exceptions, a client should not take possession of the artwork until it is completely paid for.

As an artist, I keep records of people who are buying my work on time. When they send a payment, I acknowledge with a postcard and an accounting. When the painting is paid for, I see that it is delivered to them promptly.

WHAT SELLING ART REQUIRES

Selling art can be thought of as an art. Indeed, it requires creative thinking just as creating art does. Imagination, reason, emotional involvement, good judgment, commitment, expertise, finesse, and skill are all involved in the selling process. Most artists find the thought of selling their work way outside their willingness to participate. But I have found that the process of selling art can be fun, creative, exciting, and exhilarating. I believe it has made me a better painter and put me in charge of my own career as an artist.

DEFINITION

The "art of selling art" is simply the process of developing rapport with a potential, qualified client who will benefit from owning or using the art you represent and then having the client commit to making a buying decision.

One of the most effective ways to complete a sale is to engage in a dialogue with the potential client in which you ask questions that will lead to a buying decision. Representatives who are not trained in selling art usually try to tell their clients about the works they represent. Remember, "telling is not selling!" My experience has taught me that clients might politely listen for a minute or so, but as the representative continues to talk, they become more and more disinterested. By telling, you will end up losing their attention and of course the sale as well.

People don't like to be told. People would rather tell you. So the way to get your clients really interested in owning what you have to sell is to ask them questions so that they can tell you their thoughts. The more they tell you, the more interested they will become.

ENERGY

Selling requires energy. If you have good, positive energy, people will want to do business with you. If you have a strong, healthy body, a clear mind and plenty of energy, you will feel good and be able to accomplish anything you focus your attention on. It is difficult for a tired, burned-out person to be successful. Take responsibility for your physical, emotional, and mental well-being so that you can accomplish your goals. Your energy level is dependent on these three, and all three are dependent on each other.

PHYSICAL

Physical energy is the vital energy of your body. We replenish this energy with food, sleep, rest, exercise, and body movement.

EMOTIONAL

Emotional energy is the basis for your enthusiasm, which will help you sell art. It is the energy that gives you positive feelings for life, love, happiness, and a general feeling of joy to be alive. We can keep our emotional energy strong by learning to handle our negative emotions. Learn to have an APMA—anything's possible mental attitude. Negative emotions deplete emotional energy as well as our physical and mental energies. We need to develop good emotional habits to keep our energy strong. Just one upset while you are driving a car can significantly lower your energy level for the day.

MENTAL

Your mental energy determines your creativity, thought patterns, problem solving and decision-making skills. We keep our mental power alert and efficient by getting enough sleep, meditating, and doing mental and physical exercises.

All of these energy states of being are related. If you have negative emotional energy, then your physical and mental energy will suffer. If you burn up a lot of physical energy, you will have little energy left to be creative. We must work to find and maintain an energy balance with our physical, emotional and mental states. Sensible eating, enough sleep, good daily exercise and adequate rest will help keep our energy levels high. If we don't feel good, we won't be able to sell art the way we would like.

If you lose a sale, let it go. Don't let it affect you emotionally. Know that you will close a certain proportion of your sales, but not every one. When you don't sell to someone, let it be an opportunity to learn.

A feeble body enfeebles the mind.
Jean-Jacques Rousseau

CHAPTER SUMMARY

❑ The closing question asks clients in a direct way to own or invest in the art they are admiring. The answer to a closing question will either seal the agreement or raise an objection.

❑ It is always a good idea to test close a sale before you go to the close.

❑ A test close can also help you get qualifying information about your client.

❑ Most sales will not take place unless a closing question is asked.

❑ A closing question should slip out naturally. Ask it with a smile when rapport is very high. Remain silent until you hear the answer—no matter how long it takes.

❑ One of the most powerful ways to close a sale is to change the focus of the customer's thinking away from the decision of yes or no, and instead to the ownership and enjoyment of the piece.

❑ When you are closing a sale, remain neutral to the outcome.

❑ Be mindful of your body posture and the position of your hands.

❑ Don't assist people in making a decision they will later regret.

❑ Always be closing. Make each step of the selling process a step toward closing the sale.

❑ If a person takes a work of art and hangs it in his office or home for a few days, he will most likely want to keep it.

❑ If you are going to loan art on trial, be sure to get payment first (or at least swipe a valid credit card).

❑ If you need storage space, ask friends who like your work if they would like to hang some of your art. They may end up buying it from you.

❑ Renting art can be a way of increasing your month-to-month income while the client falls in love with the work.

❑ Be sure that all lease or month-to-month rental agreements are in writing.

❑ Never think of selling art as a chore. Selling art is fun, creative, exciting and exhilarating.

❑ Don't let a lost sale deplete your energy.

❑ Orient your thinking to ways to develop a loyal clientele who will buy from you again and again.

Chapter 10
Overcoming Objections

Five steps to overcoming objections

Emotion vs. reason

I want to think it over

Cost concerns

Managing common objections

Handling rejection

When dealing with people, let us remember we are not dealing with creatures of logic. We are dealing with creatures of emotion, creatures bristling with prejudices and motivated by pride and vanity. Dale Carnegie

FIVE STEPS TO OVERCOMING OBJECTIONS

Think of objections as concerns, not obstacles.

There is nothing like the frustration that comes when you know that the person wants to own the painting and you don't seem to be able to help them take it. You feel helpless.

Handling objections and closing are closely intertwined in the selling process. They are the reasons people buy art and the reasons they don't. Answering one or more objections is often critical to making a sale. You can answer an objection and close the sale simultaneously.

OBJECTIONS ARE YOUR FRIENDS

It is rare for a person not to object to something. That is what selling is all about. Be ready for the objections. And when you hear them say, "Great!" They are fully involved. They really want the artwork! Now your job is to make it possible for them to agree to take it. So listen to their objections. Really listen! Ask them to elaborate if it is not clear. Let your clients know that you are interested in finding out how they think and feel. Repeat the objection back to them so they will know that you have listened to them and understood. Then offer an answer to the objection. Give them an alternative way to look at it. Make a suggestion that will remove the objection. Then go on and close your sale. You both will be glad you did.

Often an objection can be turned into a reason for buying. Think of objections as concerns, not obstacles. If you can emphasize the reason for buying and eliminate the objection, the sale can then happen naturally.

Listen for the reason why a client will buy and go with that. At the same time, listen for the primary reason why the client may not buy and avoid or eliminate that.

➤ **Hear it out.** Be sure to listen to your client's complete reason for not going ahead. Remember, the "I want to think it over" ploy is just a tactic we all use to end the conversation and get out of there!

➤ **Feed it back.** When you let your clients know that you have really listened to them, they will respect you more. The best way to do that is to give their objection back to them in your own words.

➤ **Question it.** At this stage, you are questioning the objection to be sure that you understand what they are saying. They are giving up the opportunity to own this artwork. Do they really want to do that? Are they going to be sorry later? Many pieces of art are originals. There is no other. They must understand that they may not have this opportunity again.

➤ **Answer the question.** Here is your opportunity to show the client that it is a good idea to go ahead. Review what has already been established. Use your creativity and resourcefulness to answer the objection

➤ **Go on and close.** Yes, it is no use answering this objection and others that may surface if you don't go on and ask for the close of the sale. After you have answered an objection, you must now ask a closing question. If another objection comes up, then you need to repeat the above process.

Mastery is not something that strikes in an instant, like a thunderbolt, but a gathering power that moves steadily through time, like the weather.
John Champlin Gardner Jr

EMOTION VS. REASON

You are not beaten until you admit it.
George S Patton Jr

It has been said that first people own, then they buy. People justify their decision to own with their reasons. People buy art with their emotions.

➤ They buy what they like.

➤ They buy what inspires them.

➤ They buy what moves them.

➤ They buy what connects to them.

➤ They buy what makes them feel good.

ASKING THE RIGHT QUESTIONS

Often when clients feel a strong emotional connection to artwork, they will want to own it. By asking the right questions, you can help involve your clients emotionally in a work of art. This is much easier than trying to help clients overcome their objections. Objections are often based on reason. Emotions generally win over reason. When you know that your clients are emotionally involved, it is far easier to help them rationalize the decision to own. And, of course, this is done by asking the right questions.

In most cases, people will buy art because of the emotional connection, but they also want to rationalize their decision with their reason. So it is important that you, as the salesperson, have a number of good reasons why the person is buying the artwork. The client needs these reasons to help rationalize spending his money and to keep from having buyer's remorse after the sale has been made. Otherwise, you will be returning the money the next day.

As a salesperson, you need to do your homework. If you are an artist selling your own work, you already know these answers. You need to be familiar with and ready to ask and answer questions on the following topics:

Medium	Style	Technique
Published articles	Important reviews	Museum shows
Gallery shows	Corporate shows	Public art shows
Artist's awards	Museum collections	

Government collections

Other collections, corporate and private

These are the most important facts you need to have available to share with your clients while they are becoming emotionally involved. Have published material—copies of newspaper and magazine reviews, brochures, books and cards—available to hand to your clients when reviewing this information.

EXERCISE

Go over the above list and fill in the information for each artist you represent. If you are representing yourself, go through the list and make a note of the most important information for each category. You don't need to tell your clients everything—just enough to help them know that they are getting a work by a recognized or established artist. People want to feel that the artwork they are buying will appreciate in value, even though the chance of ever selling it is small.

I WANT TO THINK IT OVER

When the eyes say one thing, and the tongue another, a practiced man relies on the language of the first.
Ralph Waldo Emerson

How do you answer the "I want to think it over" statement? When you hear this, your client is really saying "Goodbye." You know from your own experience that a person doesn't think it over and get back to you. It is estimated that one-half of the people who say this are ready to buy. They just need a nudge. When people are making buying decisions, they get uneasy, tense and afraid they will make a mistake. For some people, it is a traumatic situation for them to be spending so much money on a non-essential luxury purchase. You don't really expect them to take some time to think it over with their bank statements and a calculator. At the same time, if you allow them to "get away," you will likely never be so close to having this chance with them again. When the water in the tea kettle on the stove is hot, that is the time to make the tea. The next day, the water will be just as cold as it was before you turned on the heat. People are the same way.

Next time you hear this:

Client: "I want to think it over." (The client is really saying, "Goodbye.")

Answer:

Salesperson: "Oh, you want to think it over? (smile in agreement) That's a good idea. This will be a valuable art purchase for you, and you don't want to rush into it." (I like to emphasize that this purchase will be valuable for the client. Art can add value to a person's life.)

This will help your clients mentally relax. As you say this, you may want to be removing the painting from the viewing-room wall and putting it back on the gallery or studio wall. Your clients will assume that you are ending the presentation and their resistance will drop. They may even feel a little sad that they have not gone ahead and made the purchase. They realize that the artwork they have been admiring and wanting is going back on the wall and will be available for another buyer. They are losing their chance to own that piece. It's not unusual for them to change their mind at this point and decide to take it. If they really wanted the piece, they will feel a loss, especially if they had already imagined themselves owning the piece.

At this point ask:

Salesperson: "I'm curious. Obviously you have a good reason to want to think it over. May I ask what it is?"

This is a test close. You must remain perfectly silent, just as you would for a closing question. Or you might say to them:

Salesperson: "I'm sure you have a good reason for wanting to think this over. Is it the money?"

Remain silent, smile, and wait for the answer. In most cases, the person will say:

Client: "Yes, I'm concerned about the cost."

or

Client: "No, it's not the money."

COST CONCERNS

Know and understand your pricing.

The main reason for a person not to buy is "the money." If the answer is the cost or "the money," immediately go to a series of questions to deal with price concerns. Ask questions like this:

"What do you mean exactly?"

"Why do you say that?"

"Why do you feel that way?"

"Is the price your only concern?"

"Is there something else?"

"How far apart are we?"

These are great questions to ask. Any of the above questions will get the conversation moving again in the direction of closing the sale. Once your client has sufficiently answered the above questions, she will be more open to going ahead. If she is truly in love with the piece, help her own it.

When your client tells you what her concern is, you can decide if you want to continue to sell the piece. The concerns may be legitimate—not just normal buyer's reluctance to part with the money. You don't want to sell to someone who truly is going to regret the purchase afterwards. Although this is rare, it has happened to me. In one case, I returned their money the following day when they came back to me and told me that they really could not afford the second purchase they had made from me the evening before.

If you decide that they really want to own the piece and it is just a matter of finding the right terms that will help them agree to the purchase, go ahead and finish answering the objection by asking another closing question.

If the client answers:

Client: "No, it's not the money."

Ask:

Salesperson: "May I ask what it is?"

Remain silent, smile, and wait for the answer. When the person finally tells you the real concern, hear it out, feed it back, question it, and then satisfy this final condition and close the sale.

It is a good idea to practice these responses with a friend so that you will be ready when the situation arises. There is nothing like the feeling you get when you don't know how to respond. Hopefully, this book will give you the confidence you need to make those sales you have been losing when people say to you, "I want to think it over."

PHRASES TO JUSTIFY THE PRICE

One of the most frequent objections people use is, "It costs too much." Or they say, "It is more than I can afford." Many people want to buy a work of art but don't want to spend so much money, or they find it difficult to justify spending so much money on a luxury item. Art, particularly original works by renowned artists, can be expensive. The following are examples of phrases you can use to justify the price.

"Why pay $_____ for a print when, for a few dollars more, you can own an original?"

"A _____ like this is for people who can have whatever they want."

"If you have expensive tastes, you will want to own a _____."

"Isn't it better to spend a little more now on an original _____, instead of a lot more later?"

"This _____ may cost more than a _____, but it's worth much more."

"This original costs so much more than a print by the same artist, but it is the only one there is."

"This _____ is very reasonably priced at $_____."

"If you like, we can send you a monthly statement of just $_____."

"Taking care of the full amount now will save you money."

"Isn't it worth paying the price for something you really want?"

"Why don't you get it? You are worth it."

"You probably thought you couldn't afford an original _____."

"You're paying for the quality, originality, the exclusivity, and of course the name and recognition (or reputation)."

"Why don't you allow yourself a little luxury?"

"Art is a luxury that can be within anyone's reach."

"This _____ is a luxury that is not within everyone's reach."

"It's not as expensive as you may think."

"It's the Rolls Royce of ____."

"It's flagrantly expensive!"

"Don't you deserve the best?"

"Life is worth living well."

MANAGING COMMON OBJECTIONS

Here are some sample dialogues for the really tough common objections. Remember the five steps to handling objections outlined previously.

➤ Hear it out.

➤ Feed it back.

➤ Question it.

➤ Answer the question.

➤ Go on and close.

Avoid the negatively charged words—such as price, cost, buy or sell.

I ONLY BUY OILS—I'M NOT INTERESTED IN WATERCOLORS

Client: "I never buy watercolors."

Salesperson: "May I ask why?"

Client: "Sure, that's easy. Oil is more permanent."

Salesperson: "Did you know that oil paintings crack and peal when they become old, dry and brittle? That is not true of a watercolor. Watercolors, when framed and cared for properly, will last many lifetimes. Look at JMW Turner. Paintings he did 200 years ago are just as fresh as when he painted them. The ancient Egyptians painted on paper, and their pieces are still intact today. These watercolors are painted on the finest cotton rag archival paper. They will last for many, many generations."

Client: "But watercolors are not considered fine art. It's kids stuff."

Salesperson: "You are right. Watercolor is used in elementary schools to introduce painting to kids, primarily because it dries quickly and uses a water base; much less messy than oil paint. However, did you know that watercolor is a very accepted medium in the art world? The Chinese painters have used ink and watercolor for many centuries. Paul Cezanne's late work was based on his watercolor painting experience. Vincent Van Gogh painted with watercolor. Winslow Homer is more famous for his watercolors than his oils. The Metropolitan Museum of Art in New York City has over 400 of John Singer Sargent's watercolors. In short, watercolor is not just a medium for beginners. It takes great skill to find your way as a painter in watercolor. Because of the medium's spontaneity, many oil painters will tell you that watercolor is too difficult for them. Now, will you consider owning this watercolor that you have fallen in love with?"

Client: "I didn't know that watercolors were so highly regarded."

Salesperson: "Yes, Nolde, Prendergast, Whistler, Chagall, Picasso, Toulouse-Lautrec, Andrew Wyeth all painted in watercolor. Can you imagine what those are worth today?"

Client: "Wow. I'm sold on this watercolor. I'm going to get it."

Salesperson: "Congratulations!"

You can use a similar approach for selling prints on paper rather than oil paintings. If you have some knowledge of art history and famous painters, you can use this information to educate your client and sell art.

IT COSTS TOO MUCH

This is probably the most common objection. It is good to have at least two or three ready answers to this objection. Look at the list of phrases to justify price given earlier in this chapter. The following is one of my favorites.

Client: "It costs too much."

Salesperson: "It is too much? You mean that it is more than you would like."

Client: "Yes, it costs more than I can afford."

Salesperson: "May I ask you how much more it is than what you would like it to be?"

Client: "Oh, I don't know. I guess it is about $1000 more than I would like."

I have used the following exercise effectively to close sales. It simply puts the money in perspective to the artwork's value.

Salesperson: "Let's try this. Would you take this calculator?"

(Hand the calculator to your client. Always let the client do the math. It gets her actively involved. If you say something, the client may doubt you; but if the client says it, it is true.)

Salesperson: "Please punch in $1000.

Client: "Okay."

Salesperson: "Now let's assume that you will be enjoying this work of art for the rest of your time on earth. Let's estimate what that might be. Would you say another 30 or 40 years?"

Client: "That sounds good."

Salesperson: "Which?"

Client: "Let's say 30 years."

Salesperson: "Good. Why don't you divide $1000 by 30. What do you get?"

Client: "$33.34."

Salesperson: "Would you say that you will be enjoying this painting for 50 weeks a year?

Client: "Yes."

Salesperson: "Good, now please divide the $33.34 by 50. What do you get?

Client: "66 cents."

Salesperson: "Let's take it down to the day. What do you get when you divide .66 by 7?

Client: "About 10 cents."

Salesperson: "Doesn't that make it sound more manageable? I would imagine that you don't want to give up being able to own and enjoy this great artwork for just 10 cents a day, do you?

Client: "Well . . . when you put it that way, it doesn't seem so bad."

Salesperson: "Sometimes we just have to put things in their proper perspective, don't you agree?"

Client: "I guess so."

Salesperson: "Shall we go ahead with the paperwork?"

Client: "Okay."

Salesperson: "Congratulations!" (Shake the client's hand.)

This technique can be used with the amount more than the client wants to pay and also with the entire purchase price. Either way, it is effective. Notice that the salesperson never uses negatively charged words.

IT WON'T FIT THE DÉCOR OF MY HOME

Whatever the décor of the person's home or office, most art will fit in when framed or mounted properly to complement the décor. Suggest this to the client. If the client still hesitates, suggest that you demonstrate how great it will look by actually taking the piece and hanging it in the home or office. Here is another way to handle the objection:

Salesperson: "Art has a unique way of integrating perfectly with the environment in which it is placed. Just think of how wonderful the great abstract painters' works look in the old, traditional exhibition spaces of the New York Metropolitan Museum."

I'VE NEVER HEARD OF THIS ARTIST

Client: "But, I've never heard of him."

Salesperson: "That's exactly why you want to acquire one of his originals today. He is considered an emerging artist. I know of a person who picked up four Andrew Wyeth paintings in the 1950's for $50 each, when no one was paying any attention to him. Can you imagine what those paintings are worth today?"

Client: "Wow, I can imagine they are worth millions."

Salesperson: "Exactly. And that is the reason you are attracted to this man's imagery. You have a good eye for art. You can be sure that years from now these paintings are going to be very valuable. Just because you have never heard of the artist is not a reason to pass up owning a work that you love, don't you agree?

Client: "Good point."

Salesperson: "Is it yours?"

Client: "Okay, I'll take it."

Salesperson: "Congratulations. You have made an excellent decision!"

I LOVE IT, BUT MY WIFE (HUSBAND, PARTNER, ETC.) DOESN'T LIKE IT

This is a very common objection. One wants it but the other doesn't.

Client: "I really like it, but my wife doesn't feel drawn to it."

Salesperson: "That's normal. Art is a very personal experience. It is rare for two people to both be enthusiastic about the same piece. Why don't you each select something that you really like? I can tell you it will be almost impossible to find something that you both love just as much. You might find something that you both like and can live with. But why don't you both get what you really want?"

IT'S TOO COLORFUL, STRONG, SUBTLE, DRAMATIC, LARGE, SMALL, ETC.

There always seems to be something the client doesn't think is right. But you know that he wants to own the piece and will thank you in the end for helping him get it. Whatever the objection, always agree and then show him how to see the very characteristic that he is objecting to in a positive light. For example:

The objection:	You say:
Too colorful	"In your home it will become a dramatic focal point."
Too strong	"In your office it will be a symbol of the strength of your business."
Too subtle	"That is exactly what draws you in. It will become a conversation piece."
Too dramatic	"It will add energy to your environment."
Too large	"Live dangerously! People will admire you for your audacity to hang this in your home."
Too small	"With a good-sized frame, it will be a very important piece of art in your collection."

Don't be put off by objections.

Objections can help you give your clients just what they love. They are just trying to rationalize spending all that money. They want you to tell them that it is all right! No matter what the objection, there is always a good answer. Don't be discouraged when someone gives you an objection. Be appreciative and then use your creativity to come up with the appropriate answer.

EXERCISE

Write down the objections that you most frequently hear. Then write 10 different answers to each objection. You will then be prepared the next time you hear the objections.

OBJECTION _____

RESPONSES _____

_____
_____
_____
_____
_____
_____
_____
_____
_____

OBJECTION _____

RESPONSES _____

_____
_____
_____
_____
_____
_____
_____
_____
_____

In the middle of difficulty lies opportunity.
Albert Einstein

OBJECTION _____

RESPONSES _____

_____
_____
_____
_____
_____
_____
_____
_____
_____

CHAPTER SUMMARY

❑ Usually, you will need to work through at least one objection before closing a sale. When you hear an objection, you know you are almost there.

❑ It is possible to answer an objection and close the sale simultaneously.

❑ Here are the five steps to overcoming an objection:

Hear it out.

Feed it back.

Question it.

Answer the question.

Go on and close.

❑ If you want to sell more art, you need to practice overcoming objections. Question and respond to objections until the sale is complete.

❑ Practice some of the phrases in this chapter with a friend until you feel comfortable using them.

❑ Write out scripts relative to objections that you frequently hear. Then you will be ready the next time you hear one.

❑ Don't be put off by objections.

Chapter 11
After the Sale

Referrals

Thank-you notes

Why not go out on a limb? Isn't that where the fruit is?   Frank Skully

REFERRALS

One of the best ways to expand your client list is to ask for referrals when you sell art to a new client. The best time to do that is right after the sale has been made. It is a time when you and your new client feel relieved that the "business" of purchasing the art is finished and the enjoyment of the piece begins. The client feels lucky to own the work. Most likely your rapport with the client will be very high, and she will be happy to give you a referral.

ASK KINDLY AND WITH A SMILE

Salesperson: "By the way, Judy, do you know anyone from your country club who might also like to own a work by (name the artist)?"

You know what to do. Yes, you wait for an answer. Don't interrupt. Give your client some time to think about your question. Asking for a person in a specific category—the country club—makes your question easier to answer. You can change categories depending upon your client. Some other categories to consider are: your office, your department, your garden club, your health club, your bridge club, your book club, your tennis club, etc.

If she gives you a name, thank her. Then ask if she would mind recommending you to her friend. Find out when they will see each other the next time and then follow up with her with a phone call after that time. If she is very enthusiastic, she may even agree to call the friend right then and there on the spot. That is the best you can do. Then make an appointment. Follow up.

The following is a sample dialogue:

Salesperson: "So you are now the proud owner of an original Dvořák. How does it feel?"

Client: "Well, it feels great! I can't wait to get it home and hang it. I know just where it will go."

Salesperson: "I'm so glad that you are happy with your painting. Is there anyone from your tennis club that might be interested in owning a work of art? Or can you think of someone who would appreciate being on my mailing list?"

Client: "Why yes, I can think of two different individuals right now. I would be happy to refer them to you."

Salesperson: "You don't suppose that I could get you to call them to introduce me?"

Client: "Why not?"

Salesperson: "Do you think that they would be home right now?"

Client: "Let's try."

If you think that the above conversation is unrealistic, it isn't. The client is very pleased. She is grateful for the attention and care that she has received. And she has just been presented with an add-on gift that she was not expecting. She is happy to give you a couple of referrals. She is proud of her purchase and wants her friends to know her good taste and judgment in buying this art. She likes you and wants to introduce her friends.

If it turns out that you are the person making the call, you will introduce yourself with the name of the client who referred you. Tell the story of her happy purchase and then ask for an appointment. If you don't get an appointment, ask if the person would like to be on your mailing list for future shows and exhibitions. The next time you have an exhibition, give him a personal telephone invitation.

I was living in the San Francisco Bay Area. I took a trip to Los Angeles and showed my work to an art gallery there. The owner didn't say no, but she didn't say yes, either. A year later, I visited the gallery again and showed the owner more work. She said that she knew "someone" who she thought might be interested in seeing my work, someone who she thought would be interested in working with me. She was vague about the connection. She suggested that I send her some slides. I prepared the slides, a cover sheet and cover letter and sent them off, but I heard nothing. A year after that, I traveled to Los Angeles and dropped in again at the same gallery. The slides I had sent were sitting on top of a file cabinet. She said the same thing again. She knew someone, etc. I said, "Would you call them for me?" She said she would. Then I said, "Would you call them for me now, while I am here?" She walked to the phone, called, and made an appointment for me the following day. It was an art poster publisher, and yes, they liked the work. That referral turned into a published poster and a one-man show at a very well-known Southern California art museum. It would never have happened if I hadn't asked for the referral and then asked for some action on the spot.

THANK-YOU NOTES

If you make a sale to one of the people your client referred, send a thank-you note to your client.

"Thank you so much for referring me to Mr. Artcollector. He acquired a painting from me for his office this week. Enclosed is a token of my appreciation."

Include a small print, a beautiful poster or even a small painting—something you know your client will appreciate and value. You may also suggest that the next time she selects a painting from you, she will get a 10% discount as a way of saying thank you for the referrals. Give her an added incentive to keep in touch and to buy more art from you.

There is so much to do to be successful in this business It is sometimes very hard to do everything you know you "should" do. But there is one thing that is a must. Follow up with a thank-you note on a sale, a client meeting, a gallery appointment, a referral, or any situation where someone gave you time, energy or money.

THE THREE PRINCIPLES OF A GOOD THANK-YOU NOTE

➤ Say what it is for.

➤ State how it has benefited you.

➤ Offer something in return.

A thank-you note is a brief, appropriate and sincere expression of appreciation. That is the primary intention. If possible, try to offer something in return.

A thank-you note adds heart to the cold world of business. And, since a lot of art and artists come from the heart, a sincere note of appreciation is never out of place in the art world. Gallery owners, businesspeople, artists, and everyone else will remember thank-you notes and the people who sent them. If you visit a gallery for the purpose of seeking representation, send the gallery and the person you spoke with a thank-you note. If a client comes into your gallery and is sincerely interested in owning a work of art, send a thank-you note. If you write a gallery for information on how to submit work and the gallery responds by sending you application materials and guidelines, send a thank-you note.

By nature, a thank-you note is brief. It is not a letter.

146

EXAMPLES OF THANK-YOU NOTES

Salesperson: "The gallery staff and I want to tell you how much we have appreciated working with your company these past few weeks. Thank you for your collaboration and confidence. Please accept this small token of our appreciation"

Artist: "Thank you for taking the time to look at my portfolio. Your insightful comments and kind referral have been very helpful. Please come visit the studio and pick out a gift—a small print for your office."

Gallery: "You will be pleased to know that your April art sales broke all our gallery records. It is wonderful to have you as part of our team. Please accept the enclosed print as a token of my appreciation."

Client: "Just a note to tell you how much we enjoyed working with your staff person, Judy Seller. She was so attentive to our needs and we are delighted with our new art piece. Please visit for a glass of wine and see how beautiful our _____ looks in our living room."

Art rep: "I want to thank you for your recent acquisition for your outstanding art collection. Your enthusiasm for art is infectious. We at _____ Gallery want you to know that you may have a 10% discount on any art you obtain from our gallery in the future."

As you read the above thank-you notes, you can see how each reflects my three principles for a good thank-you note.

INDIVIDUALIZED THANK-YOU STATIONARY

When I send a thank-you note, I either send some small, original work of art or a nice card from my collection. Use your creative thinking to find a unique way to send a note of thanks.

Only by giving are you able to receive more than you already have.
Jim Rohn

CHAPTER SUMMARY

❑ The best time to ask for a referral is right after a sale has taken place.

❑ Ask the person giving the referral if she will make the call for you.

❑ If you are calling the referral, introduce yourself with the name of the person who referred you. Mention that the person has just become the proud owner of an original work of art.

❑ When you make a sale to a referred client, send a thank-you note and a gift to the person who referred you.

❑ Keep thank-you notes brief and to the point.

❑ Make thank-you notes upbeat and personal in tone.

❑ Use the person's name on a thank-you note.

❑ Send a small gift with the thank-you note.

Chapter 12
Sale Venues

Art fairs

Open studios

The viewing room

Networking

Gallery floor selling

There is only one thing to be said at an opening: You say congratulations.
Louise Bourgeois

ART FAIRS

People who attend outdoor art fairs think that they are not paying gallery prices. However, if you also sell in a gallery, you will have to sell your work for comparable prices at the art fair or in your studio. You can't undersell your gallery if you want to keep exhibiting your work with the gallery.

COMMITMENT AND PREPARATION

Art fairs are a great place to sell your art. I know artists who support themselves very well doing art fairs.

Don't begin to sell at art fairs unless you intend to do a lot of them. It will take you three or four fairs before you begin to get your technique down. Don't give up if you have a poor weekend. Art fairs require a lot of preparation and a real commitment of time during the fair, as well as a lot of creative thinking. Plan, plan, and plan some more. There is packing and preparation time, travel time, set-up time, chatting-with-the-public time, selling time, take-down time. I have a lot of respect for artists who sell at art fairs, and I try to support them by purchasing something when I attend. I used to do art fairs, but I just don't have the time anymore.

PRACTICE YOUR SELLING SKILLS

Art fairs are an excellent venue to practice your selling skills. You will have literally hundreds of opportunities to practice selling. If you really want to learn to sell your work, I recommend doing 25-50 art fairs. At the end of that time, you will have developed a personal selling style that relates perfectly to the work you produce.

You must be willing to be with the public—all kinds of people. You will hear everything about your work. Sometimes people are unkind, outspoken, or rude. Others will be enthusiastic, supportive, or appreciative. Treat everyone with respect. Don't judge people by how they look or what they say. Art fairs are a real lesson in human nature. You will be surprised that people whom you would never expect to buy from you end up doing just that. You will meet a lot of people, some of whom will become your loyal collectors. Make everyone feel important—they are.

Develop your easy conversation skills and questions. Learn how to pull people into your 10x10' gallery space. Have a painting, a print, or a poster that is an eyecatcher. I used to use my *King of Beasts* poster to attract people's attention. If you want to see it, look at my web site: www.youcreate.com. You will see why it grabbed people's attention. Remember that you are competing with all the other booths. Ask yourself why people will want to come and look at your art.

Crafts usually do very well at art fairs, especially wearable items such as clothes and jewelry. If you create these items, art fairs may be very profitable for you.

LOOK GOOD AND SMILE A LOT

Wear clean and neat clothes. Kid around with people. Keep it light and fun. If people like you, they will buy from you.

NICE LOOKING BOOTH

Your booth should look like a small gallery. Have inexpensive merchandise—prints or posters—available. You can have bargain bins for people to browse through as a way of getting people involved.

HAVE ASSISTANCE

Be sure you have someone to relieve you. You will have to take breaks. Don't eat in your booth; have someone else watch your booth while you eat lunch. The booth is for selling and promotion, and that is all. Think of a booth at an art fair as a mini open studio.

Pick the best art fairs in your area. If they are juried, send in your applications. If you get in and do well, there is a good chance you will be invited back the next year. Some artists travel around the country in their vans all summer, doing art fairs. Then they produce more work during the fall, winter and spring for the next summer's art fairs. This is one way of making a living as an artist.

It is good to have a wide price range, between $25 and $10,000. Most sales will most likely be under $1,000. You will also have to be set up to accept credit cards.

TIPS

☛ Make your booth look like a small gallery.

☛ Have some inexpensive pieces, perhaps a bargain bin.

☛ Have plenty of business cards to hand out.

☛ Ask a visitor, "What kind of artwork do you collect?"

☛ Never sit in your booth.

☛ Never read a book in your booth.

☛ Wearing a name tag can be a friendly thing to do.

OPEN STUDIOS

One of the least expensive and best ways for an artist to sell artwork is during an open studio. I know a number of artists who support themselves for the entire year on just one open studio event. If you do it right, and you have high-quality art to sell, you can do very well. The best place to have an open studio is in or near a metropolitan area. The San Francisco Bay Area, where I have my studio, has many open studio events. Each area has an organized open-studio art tour that is sponsored by an open-studio art organization and takes place over three or four weekends. The art tour organizer has a mailing list of interested buyers that they have collected over the years, and they do a huge mailing to publicize the event with a brochure and map to direct buyers to individual art studios. They also publicize the event in the local newspaper. For a fee, an artist can be included in this brochure and have her studio noted on the map. Artists who are serious and ready to sell their work know that the fee is well worth it.

OPEN STUDIO PUBLICITY

Send out your own open-studio announcements two to three weeks before the event. I have a list of names and addresses on the computer. My office assistant prints out address labels. It is fairly easy to get a postcard printed up with a color image and your open-studio announcement on the other side. Use an image of a work that is for sale. I have used www.modernpostcard.com many times and find that they give good, timely service and their prices are very competitive. If you can't afford a printer for color postcards, improvise on your computer and use a copy service to print your cards. Use your creativity to find the least expensive way to do an invitation that will be eye-catching.

YOUR MAILING LIST

Keep all your friends, relatives, past clients, referral clients, and interested people in one mailing-list file. Also include local newspaper reviewers, local museum curators, and your local TV station on your list. Keep these files current. When you send out a mailer, put the words "Return Service Requested" at the bottom of the address block. If it is returned, the post office will give you the new address. I also print on the announcement in very small print just under the space for the label, "Please check your address label and call, write, or e-mail with any corrections."

When people attend your open studio, have them print their names in the guest book. Have them check if they want to be notified about future open studios and gallery exhibitions. If they don't want to be notified, respect their wishes and save the postage.

PREPARING YOUR STUDIO SPACE

All of these suggestions will help create a warm and friendly atmosphere in your studio.

➤ Clean up your studio.

➤ Sweep and mop the floor.

➤ Get as much clutter put away as possible.

Many people get upset around dirt and clutter. If your studio is not inviting, some people won't want to stay very long. Since it is your studio, there is a certain amount of clutter that may have to remain, but do your best to put things away, hang up aprons, throw out old paper coffee cups and last night's pizza box. Tidy up your space and display your work in a tasteful way. If your studio has useable outside space, you may want to put up some portable walls or tables outdoors. This will expand your display options. Have a small desk and chair ready as a place to handle sales.

If you are serving food and beverages, have them on a separate table away from the art. A good food aroma can add to the ambiance of the space.

Be mindful of the temperature. Keep your studio warm enough so that people will be comfortable and will want to stay to look at your art. Many studios are cool or cold. Buy a portable heater if you don't have good heating. People won't want to stay if their feet and hands are cold.

Have appropriate music playing. Choose carefully what you play and keep the volume low. Turn off the music if it becomes too much to hold a conversation.

Have your work well lit. Make sure that people can see what you are selling in the best light. You most likely won't have a viewing room, but you can improvise. I have a large painting easel in my studio that I use during my open-studio events as a viewing place. I have a moveable desk lamp attached to the easel, and I can place a painting on the easel and light it from above with the desk lamp.

Clutter will distract buyers from seeing the work.

Before I had my own studio space, I used to have open studios in my home. We carried the furniture out of the living room and put it on the back patio; the living room became the art gallery. Artworks were displayed on the walls and tables. The dining space was used to serve food and beverages. Since it was always December, we served warm, spiced red wine and cheese, ham and crackers, which added a pleasant aroma to the environment.

If you don't have a studio and you want to organize a kind of open-studio event, you can ask someone—a friend or relative—to rent you a space for this kind of event. You can even offer to barter for the space with some of your artwork.

ASSISTANCE

You will need to get some help during your open-studio hours. Either hire a professional to come and work with you, or if you don't want to pay another person, ask a friend or relative to assist you. You need at least one other person to help you manage the sales. Artists who already have art representatives working with them may want to have the representatives present during the event. Whoever helps you, be sure that he or she is aware of your pricing and discount policies. If the person has never sold art before, I suggest you go over some of the material in this book together so that both of you are knowledgeable about selling art.

SUPPORTING MATERIAL

During the open studio, have available next to your sign-in book your business card, brochures featuring you and your work, and any postcards or posters that you have to promote your work. People like to take away something to remind them of you and your artwork. Your brochure needs to have a list of the collections that own your work, a list of your one-person or group shows and exhibitions, and your gallery representation (if you have it). The postcards and posters are for sale or to give away with other materials.

BARGAIN TABLE

A couple of years ago, I tried the idea of putting out a pile of small demonstration watercolors—6x 9"—that I had done in the many watercolor classes I teach. I packaged each in a clear plastic bag and put out a sign that said, "Anything in this pile - $5.00." For $50, a person could walk away with 10 pieces. They sold so fast, I am thinking of raising the price to $10.00 next time. One woman bought 18. Think about what you might put on your "bargain" table.

GIVE SOMETHING AWAY

When I have an open studio, besides giving away my promotional material I always like to have an art piece of some kind to give away to the people who take the trouble to come. Even if they don't buy, I offer them a black and white poster to take home with them. I think that it is a good practice to say thank you for coming, and a way to remember me, especially if they hang it in their house.

RED DOTS

Red dots on the title card of an artwork typically indicate "sold." If you can do some pre-sales and have red dots on some of your pieces, it will entice visitors to take action. Not only do red dots evoke urgency, but they help people feel that they are making a good choice; after all, someone else bought this artist's work.

TIPS

- ☛ Include good directions to your studio on the invitation and large signs leading to the entrance on the days of the event.

- ☛ Clean your space and put away as much clutter as you can.

- ☛ Some fine rugs on the floor will make your studio look prosperous. Borrow them for the day if necessary.

- ☛ Have something interesting in your studio for children to keep them occupied, such as a fascinating book or a puzzle.

- ☛ Fresh flowers can add atmosphere and a touch of fragrance.

- ☛ Make sure that all your work is priced.

- ☛ Have bubble wrap and tape handy for carry-out framed works or sculpture.

- ☛ Smile a lot.

THE VIEWING ROOM

Many art galleries have a special room called a "viewing room." It is a quiet, private space with three or four places to sit and an easel to hold a painting or print with very warm, focused lighting directed toward the easel. These rooms are sometimes called "dimmer rooms" because they are equipped with a dimmer switch. You can control the lighting so that the client can see the painting or print in different lighting. This viewing room is also sometimes called a "closing room" because many sales are closed in this intimate environment. If you are working in a gallery that has a viewing room, you will be expected to use this space.

When clients have indicated an interest in a particular piece, you have qualified the clients, and you are reasonably sure that they are able to pay for it, take the painting or print off the gallery wall and carry it to the viewing room. The clients will object, as they always do, but they will follow you to the viewing room.

Salesperson: "Please follow me, I want you to see this with better lighting."

Client: "Oh, don't bother, we were just looking."

Salesperson: "I know you are just looking, but I want you to just look at this!"

Be creative, find the right playful words that will carry the conversation to the viewing room. Smile and enthusiastically say:

Salesperson: "Just look at this! I want you to see what happens to the light in the sky. Have a seat."

The couch or chairs in the viewing room are usually very comfortable. Once your clients sit down, they will want to stay for a while. An art gallery with a viewing room will frequently offer the client something to drink or some kind of treat.

Here are some other examples of what you can say:

Salesperson: "In the gallery the painting has to compete with all the other works. Here you can enjoy it without any distraction."

Salesperson: "In here you can see it more like it will appear in your home."

The viewing room is a great place to ask some more of the connecting questions (see Chapter 8).

EXERCISE

If you work in an art gallery, practice taking the client to the viewing room with one of your fellow sales representatives playing the part of the client. Actually take a painting off the wall and role-play with your partner. Then continue the conversation in the viewing room. Use the dimmer switch and ask questions until your partner agrees to buy the work. An exercise like this will give you the confidence you need to use the viewing room with an actual client.

TIPS

☛ A private viewing space with good lighting to view artwork will add to your success in closing sales.

☛ The viewing room together with connecting questions will help your clients decide to "own" the art.

☛ Use the viewing room to test close and close your sales.

NETWORKING

It takes 20 years to build a reputation and five minutes to lose it.
Warren Buffett

Get comfortable navigating in the art world. Although there are some real deadbeats, I hope you will discover, as I have, that the art world is generally a friendly place. Most people are helpful and have a good disposition. Always be respectful. Art gallery owners get tired of people who walk into their galleries without an appointment and ask for representation. Most have not even researched the gallery and don't know what it sells.

ART OPENINGS

A good place to network is at art gallery openings. Circulate and meet people who look interesting to you. Always make a point to meet the artists and say something original about your assessment of the work. Let them know that you have really looked at it. Many people go to art openings just for the party, to drink the wine, eat the food and meet the people. Make the people more important to you than the refreshments. Always be at your best. The best publicity you can get is by word of mouth. Your reputation will follow you.

BE PREPARED

Be prepared to talk about yourself. What do you say when someone asks:

> "What do you do?"

> "What kind of painting do you do?"

> "What medium do you work in?"

> "What kind of art do you make?"

All of these questions require a prepared short and long answer. The short answer is the one you have ready for those who are obviously in a hurry at the art opening and want to go on to meet the next person. The long answer is for the people who really want to get to know you and are interested in what you do. A very good short answer makes people want to learn more. The idea is to make a favorable and memorable impression with everyone you meet.

Here is an example of how I might answer the question, "What kind of art do you make?" when it is asked by another artist or guest. I might answer: "I create paintings in watercolor and oil in a very personal way. What kind of artist are you, Don?" That answer gives him enough information to know what medium I use and that I am not just another of the many thousands of watercolor painters. It doesn't give any details. If he wants to know more, he might say, "What do you mean by 'a personal way'?" And that would be a lead into a longer, more detailed answer. You also need to follow up to let him know that you are interested in what he does. Now you are on the way to building some rapport and connection.

When you are in a social situation, if someone asks about you, after you answer, don't forget to ask him about himself with the same amount of interest. Some artists have sizeable egos and care little about what someone else is doing. Only when they sense that there may be a personal gain in knowing you will they really become interested.

People in the art business can be very impatient for success. If you have made the commitment to be successful no matter how long it takes, it will help you be patient.

Most people that you meet can assist you in some way. It is a two-way street. You can assist most people you meet in some way. Look for ways to help others and they will try to help you.

Here is an example of a conversation I had with a businessman standing in line, waiting to board an airplane. He said to me, "What do you do?" I answered, "I am an artist, I paint watercolors in a very personal way. Do you collect art?" As it turned out, he said, "Why, yes I do. In fact, I have a collection of watercolor paintings." Again, there is the power of asking questions.

Be interested and you will be interesting.

TIPS

☞ If you want to be successful at networking, learn to be interested in people and find out how you can help them.

☞ Prepare a short and a long answer to the question, "What do you do?"

☞ Always follow up your answer with a question.

☞ Follow up with the people you have met.

GALLERY FLOOR SELLING

THE GREETING

Smile! It is important to remember this. A smile is the best ice breaker. Be friendly and kind. Be warm-hearted and sincere. Be yourself. Be genuinely interested in each person that you talk to. Try to see people with the letters M M F I—Make Me Feel Important!—on their foreheads. Treat everyone as a potential buyer. Don't judge them by how they are dressed. Treat everyone, no matter how they look, with courtesy and respect. Even if they say they are there only to look, there is a good possibility that they will go home with a work of art if you ask them the right questions. Always stay present.

When engaging a gallery visitor, you want to find out as much as you can about the person to qualify her as a potential client. The following questions will help you do that:

Salesperson: "Do you collect art?"

Salesperson: "Have you bought art before?"

If so, ask:

Salesperson: "What kind of art do you own?" (paintings, drawings, prints, sculpture, posters, old, contemporary, etc.)

If not, ask:

Salesperson: "Do you think you are ready to begin?"

Salesperson: "If you knew more about art, do you think you would be interested in owning some special works?"

Do not ask a gallery visitor—a potential client—"dead end" questions such as, "Where are you from?" "Do you know so and so?" Keep your questions on the subject of the artwork and how it relates to the client.

DON'T SAY:

May I help you? Are you an artist? Do you live in _____(this city)? Are you from out of town? Are you looking for something in a particular? Do you have any questions? Would you like to buy something? These can be worn-out questions that will more likely than not annoy the gallery visitor. Try to be original and creative.

DO SAY:

Salesperson: "Hi, welcome!" (Smile!)

Salesperson: "Welcome to the gallery!" (Smile!)

Salesperson: "Feel free to enjoy the work as long as you like."

Salesperson: "Is this your first time in the_____ Gallery?"

Client: "Why, yes!"

Salesperson: "My name is _____ _____
             (first and last name)."

Client: "My name is Judy Buyer."

Salesperson: "Is it all right if I call you Judy?" (Judy nods.)

Salesperson: "And you may call me _____. Let me
             explain how the gallery is laid out, Judy. Then I
             will leave you alone so that you can enjoy the
             works."

If this is her first time in the gallery, simply explain how the gallery
is laid out, how the work is displayed, and where she can find
everything, including the restrooms, to make her feel comfortable.
Use the person's name while you are talking. This will help you
establish good rapport right from the beginning.

THEN SAY:

Salesperson: "Enjoy the work. I'll check back with you later."

Client: "Oh, that won't be necessary."

Salesperson: "No problem. I'll check back with you. A lot of
             people come in just to look and leave with a
             painting they can't part with." (Smile.)

If she has visited the gallery before:

Client: "Why, yes, I have been here before."

Salesperson: "Then I will assume you know how the gallery is
             laid out. Is there a particular artist that you are
             looking for?"

Client: "Yes, I came to see _____'s work.

Salesperson: "Let me show you where her work is located."

Then help her to that particular artist's grouping.

If she says no and that she just wants to look around:

Salesperson: "Then I will leave you alone so that you can enjoy the art. If you have a question or would just like to chat about some particular piece, I will be here."

Be careful to keep the conversation on the artwork.

Salesperson: "If you think you might be interested in taking something home with you, please let me know so that I can assist you."

Remember, after every explanation, ask a question.

Always invite your clients to take pleasure in and enjoy the artwork displayed. Remember that your tone of voice is very important. It breaks the ice and lets a stranger off the street know that you are open, friendly, and easy to talk to. Suggest the possibility of owning a work of art. Don't be pushy or get in the way of their viewing pleasure. There is no need to volunteer more information than what they want to know. When you are asked a question, answer the question and follow up with a question—after every explanation, ask a question. Take charge and lead the way.

AFTER THE GREETING

Here are some phrases you may use after visitors have had a chance to look around:

Salesperson: "Did you come in to see a particular artist?"

"Do we have you on our mailing list?"

"Have you been in the gallery before?"

"Did you see anything that you would like to take home with you?"

Client: "Yes, of course, but I can't afford to buy any art right now."

Salesperson: "I understand. (Smile.) But did you see a particular painting that really spoke to you?"

A question like this can open up a serious conversation about a particular piece. If she is willing to show you the piece she is really attracted to, then this will allow you to begin a series of connection questions. (See Chapter 8.)

Always stand and look people in the eye when you speak to them. Never sit while there are people in the gallery. This makes you look uninterested and unavailable.

CO-OP GALLERY

If it is a co-op gallery, you may explain that the works presented on walls are works by all the members of the co-op. Each member of the co-op is responsible for the management and a percentage of the gallery expenses, and each member must take turns working as the gallery representative during business hours. Mention that you are one of the artists. Give your name. Use the same dialogues outlined in the previous "The Greeting" section. But when you introduce yourself, say:

Salesperson: "I am one of the artists exhibiting in this gallery. My name is _____ _____ " (first and last name).

This can be an opening for the visitor to ask:

Client: "Oh, is that right? May I see some of your work?"

It is really a privilege for the gallery visitor to actually meet one of the exhibiting artists. This could open the way for a sale of one of your paintings.

You may also explain that since this is a co-op gallery, when a painting is priced, there is not the same large markup as in most retail art galleries. Explain that for this reason, they can own an original painting for around half of what it would cost in a commercial retail gallery. This is an added incentive for a client to buy from a co-op gallery. It is not necessary to tell the gallery visitor what the actual breakdown percentages are.

TIPS

☛ Be genuinely interested in each person you talk to. Make each one feel important.

☛ Do not ask a gallery visitor—a potential client—"dead end" questions.

☛ Treat everyone, no matter how they look, with courtesy and respect.

☛ Remember that your tone of voice is very important. It breaks the ice and lets a stranger off the street know that you are open, friendly, and easy to talk to.

☛ Always stand and look people in the eye when you talk to them.

☛ Never sit while there are people in the gallery. This makes you look uninterested and unavailable.

☛ Always invite gallery visitors to take pleasure in and enjoy the artwork displayed.

Chapter 13
Setting Sales Goals

Successful attitude

If one thing matters, everything matters.   Wolfgang Tillmans

SUCCESSFUL ATTITUDE

Shoot for the moon. Even if you miss, you will land among the stars.
Les Brown

Your future success will be determined by your attitude at this moment. Goals will help you maintain an attitude of success. Goals are like magnets that pull you toward your desired outcomes. More important than learning how to achieve what you want is discovering what and why you want it. Once you know that, you can write down your goals. When your goals are written down, preferably in your handwriting and in the present tense, they become imbedded in your mind. Then they will manifest, so be careful what you wish for!

Begin writing your general goals down now. Ask yourself what kind of life you want, what kind of success you want to experience. Then begin writing. Don't wait. Write as many goals as you want. Write as fast as you can. Write them in the first-person present tense. I now have . . . I now am . . . I now sell . . . It is okay to have a lot of goals. Begin by writing the easy ones first, then the more difficult goals. Use the space below. Now is the best time to begin this goal-writing project.

The happiest people in the world are those who take charge of their lives. Those who take action will achieve their goals. The first step to taking action is to write down your goals.

WRITE YOUR GENERAL GOALS HERE

_____

_____

_____

_____

_____

_____

_____

_____

_____

_____

Now that you have written down your easy and not-so-easy general goals, write down your specific goals for selling art. Say what it is that you want and when you want it. Don't worry about the "how." Hows have a way of taking care of themselves when specific goals have been selected. For example: I want to begin by selling $XXXX of artwork each month. First set short-term goals, then go on to long-term goals.

MY GOALS FOR THE NEXT WEEK

_____

_____

_____

_____

_____

_____

You may not feel that you are ready to set goals. Go ahead anyway. There is no reason not to. And please don't make excuses like, "I'm too old, too young, not good-looking enough, not smart enough, too fat, too short, too busy, too lazy, don't have enough education" or any other lame excuse you can think of. You know that there are people in all these categories who have achieved unbelievable success.

MY GOALS FOR THE NEXT 30 DAYS

_____

_____

_____

_____

_____

_____

The great successful men (and women) of the world have used their imaginations; they think ahead and create their mental picture, and then go to work materializing that picture in all its details, filling in here, adding a little there, altering this bit and that bit, but steadily building, steadily building.
Robert Collier

MY GOALS FOR THE NEXT SIX MONTHS

_____

_____

_____

_____

_____

_____

_____

_____

_____

_____

_____

_____

Don't hope to achieve your goals—expect to achieve them.

It is important to visualize your goals. Picture in your mind what it will be like to achieve your goals. Goals should not be confused with wishful thinking. Goals require commitment. Set your goals and set about achieving them. Here is a four-step process for goal-setting that is inspired by Napoleon Hill's *"Six Steps that Turn Desires into Gold"* as outlined in his book, *Think and Grow Rich.*

PROCESS FOR GOAL-SETTING

➤ Write the exact goal. Be specific.

➤ Establish what exactly you are going to give or trade for what you desire—your attention, sincerity, more enthusiasm, interest, more effort, energy, work, time.

➤ Write out a single paragraph that states clearly and simply the reward or money that you intend to have; name the date by which it will be acquired. State specifically what you intend to give in return for this reward or money, and describe clearly and briefly your plan of action. Keep the paragraph as brief as possible. but do mention all the above points.

➤ Read this written statement aloud, twice daily—once upon awakening in the morning and once just before you go to sleep at night. As you read it, picture yourself already in possession of your reward or money. This is a way to get your goals into your subconscious, where they are powerful.

GOAL-SETTING

When you write down your goals, you will find yourself looking at your life in a different way. You will see yourself as you really are living in the world. You live in the universe, and the universe exists in you. There is an abundant supply of resources for everyone on the planet. It is only our thinking that keeps us limited. What we experience in life is the effect of our thoughts. When you change your thinking, you change your life. Creating goals is the easiest way to change your thinking. You want to live being the cause of your life, not being the effect of the world.

Do not fix your attention on "How." The source of your abundance is your being. The source is infinite. So set your goals on what you want, need, and on what you can do to make the world a better place.

When writing your goals, be spontaneous and true to yourself. These goals are for you, not for anyone else. You may want to write them on a separate paper and keep them private. Do everything you can to free yourself and be yourself when you write your goals.

CREATE A SELF-PORTRAIT

Paint a portrait in words. Write a biography for yourself. Pretend that you are listed in *Who's Who in America*. Write out how you want your biography to read late in your life. It should include your education, work experience, the various positions you have held, your main contributions, what you are especially known for, your main achievement, awards that you have received, other ways you have been recognized by your peers, where you live, and any other pertinent details. Edit this biography every year on your birthday.

KEEPING GOALS PRIVATE

When you share your goals with another person, you can dissipate some of your creative energy. It is best to keep goals private. If you are going to share your goals with someone, be sure that she will give you nothing but support and encouragement. Even better is if the person is willing to help you in some way move toward your goals.

Rowing harder doesn't help if the boat is headed in the wrong direction.
Kenichi Ohmae

CHAPTER SUMMARY

❑ Your goals will manifest in the future. Be careful what you wish for.

❑ The best way to establish your goals is to write them down.

❑ Don't make excuses for not setting goals. There are no excuses. Just do it.

❑ Don't worry about how your goals will become reality. The hows have a way of taking care of themselves when specific goals have been selected.

❑ Picture in your mind what it will be like to achieve each of your goals.

❑ Review your main goals often, preferably every morning and evening.

❑ Write a biography of yourself as you would like it to read late in your life.

❑ Keep your goals private. Share them only with people you know will help you achieve them.

Chapter 14
Resources

"How To" list

Client profile

Client information sheet

Communication log

It is our attitude much more than our aptitude that will determine our success.

"HOW TO" LIST

Before you take on the world as a salesperson, make a list of "how to" questions to prepare yourself. Here are sample lists of just a few of the "how to" questions you might ask. After you have listed these questions, then problem-solve your list. Write as many ideas down as you can that will answer each "how to" question.

FOR AN ARTIST

How to paint (sculpt, print, manufacture) what is to be for sale?

How to select which items are going to be for sale?

How to present the work I am going to sell? (matted, framed, glassed, varnished, etc.)

How do I decide what prices to ask for the works?

How to get the greatest number of people to view my work?

How can I get the largest number of people to sell my work?

ARTIST EXAMPLE

Next, pick the ideas you get and prioritize them. Number the ideas according to importance until your entire idea list is prioritized. Start working on the number-one item and continue until you complete all the items that you think are important. Do something every day to get you closer to your goals.

For example, take the question: How to select which items are going to be for sale? You might come up with a list like this:

Look at my entire inventory of works.

Pick out only the best works.

Select the pieces that look like they all belong to a body of work.

Decide if I am ready to let these works go.

Hold back the work that I want to keep in my own collection.

Decide if I want to make prints of any of these paintings.

Decide how many prints I will include in each edition.

Have a variety of sizes.

FOR A GALLERY SALES REP

How can I find more prospective clients?

How can I show my clients that I really care?

How can I show the kind of work people will want to own?

How do I make people comfortable when they enter the gallery?

How can I be respectful of the gallery visitors?

How can I make my gallery inviting so that people will want to stay and view the art?

How do I let people know about my gallery?

How do I let people know about the artists and the work we are showing in our gallery?

Next, pick the ideas you get and prioritize them. Number the ideas according to importance until your entire idea list is prioritized. Start working on the number-one item and continue until you complete all the items that you think are important. Do something every day to get you closer to your goals.

GALLERY REP EXAMPLE

For example, take the question: How can I make my gallery inviting so that people will want to stay and view the art? You might come up with a list like this:

Put some wonderful examples in the window of the gallery.

Make sure that a pedestrian can see into the gallery from the street.

Make the view from just inside the door very inviting.

Make sure that all the works are well lit.

Make sure that the gallery looks neat and clean.

Remove all unnecessary clutter.

Have wonderful music playing.

Make sure that the gallery smells good.

Offer gallery visitors tea or coffee.

Be sure that all the gallery staff are friendly and make visitors feel comfortable.

Give people space to be alone and view the work.

Have a comfortable viewing room that can show off one work of art to at least three people.

Have publicity available for guests.

Have recent articles and reviews mounted and displayed.

Have portfolios picturing other works by the gallery artists that are not on display.

Have the artist come and give a talk about the work.

Be sure that the artist is present at the opening.

These are samples of the kind of idea generation that can come from just one "how to" question. This process is valuable and well worth the time needed to carry it out. It really helps you get your priorities in order.

CLIENT PROFILE

Name

Address

Work phone   Home phone   Cell phone

Referred by   Age

BACKGROUND INFORMATION

Single/married/divorced   Spouse's name and age

Children and ages

Pets

Occupation

Education/income level

Type of furnishing/home style

ART PREFERENCES

Subject matter   Colors

Style/type of work   Size/medium preferred

Needs/wants

Intended use

IMPRESSIONS AND COMMENTS

Last contact date by phone

Last mailing

Needs information on

Other follow-up needs

PURCHASES

Date	Price	Size	Medium	Title/Description	Use

CLIENT INFORMATION SHEET

Name

Address

Work phone   Home phone   Cell phone

Referred by   Fax   Best time to call

COMMUNICATION LOG				
Date	Reason for contact	Commitment date	Action taken	Next date

TELEPHONE LOG

Date	Time	Notes	Follow-up

INDEX

INDEX

Mailing Lists

		PRICE PER LIST
1.	47,000 Visual Artists	$100 per 1000
2.	900 Art Councils	$80
3.	350 Art Publications	$50
4.	1700 Art Publishers	$150
4A.	900 Greeting Card Publishers	$75
4B.	130 Print Distributors	$50
4C.	350 Greeting Card Sales Reps	$50
4D.	225 Licensing Contacts	$50
4E.	180 Calendar Publishers	$50
5.	400 Book Publishers	$50
6.	535 Corporations Collecting Art	$60
6A.	160 Corporations Collecting Photography	$50
7.	750 Art Stores	$65
8.	1950 Reps, Consultants, Brokers, Dealers	$150
8A.	170 Corporate Art Consultants	$50
9.	1900 College Art Departments	$150
9A.	1900 College Galleries	$150
10.	600 Libraries	$60
11.	6500 Galleries	$80 per 1000
11A.	425 Photo Galleries	$50
11B.	800 New York City Galleries	$70
11C.	1300 California Galleries	$95
12.	550 Foreign Galleries	$70
12B.	250 Canadian Galleries	$50
13.	2500 Art Organizations and Exhibition Spaces	$170
13A.	450 Art Organization Newsletters	$60
14.	1000 Art Museums	$75
14A.	625 Art Museum Gift Store Buyers	$75
15.	800 Architects	$70
16.	700 Interior Designers	$65
17.	1900 Frame and Poster Galleries	$150

All lists can be rented for onetime use and may not be copied, duplicated or reproduced in any form. Lists have been seeded to detect unauthorized usage. Reorder of same lists within a 12-month period qualifies for 25% discount. Lists cannot be returned or exchanged.

FORMATS/CODING

All domestic names are provided in zip code sequence on three-up pressure-sensitive labels. We mail to each company/person on our list a minimum of once per year. Our business thrives on responses to our mailings, so we keep them as up-to-date and clean as we possibly can.

SHIPPING

Please allow one week for processing your order once your payment has been received. Lists are sent Priority Mail and take an additional 2-4 days. Orders sent without shipping costs will be delayed. $5 shipping per order.

GUARANTEE

Each list is guaranteed 95% deliverable. We will refund 37¢ per piece for undeliverable mail in excess of 5% if returned to us within 90 days of order.

ArtNetwork
530·470·0862   800·383·0677   530·470·0256 Fax
PO Box 1360, Nevada City, CA 95959-1360
www.artmarketing.com   <info@artmarketing.com>

Art Office

Business Forms, Charts, Sample Letters, Legal Documents and Business Plan

This book provides artists with a wide selection of indispensable business forms, charts, sample letters, legal documents and business plans . . . all for photocopying. Organize your office's administrative and planning functions. Reduce routine paperwork and increase time for your art creation.

Also available in PDF format for $14.95
(no shipping costs)

80+ forms include:

12-month planning calendar ❦ Sales agreement
Model release ❦ Rental-lease agreement ❦ Form VA
Slide reference sheet ❦ Competition record
Customer-client record ❦ Phone-zone sheet
Monthly project status form ❦ Marketing plan
12-month show planner ❦ Checklist for a juried show
Print planning calendar ❦ Bill of sale
Pricing worksheet ❦ Press release ❦ and lots more

ABOUT THE AUTHORS
Sue Viders has been a practicing artist and art consultant for over 30 years. **Constance Smith** founded ArtNetwork over 18 years ago to assist artists nationwide with their marketing.

$16.95   112 pages   ISBN: 0-940899-27-2   2003 edition $4 shipping

ArtNetwork
530·470·0862   800·383·0677   530·470·0256 Fax
PO Box 1360, Nevada City, CA 95959-1360
www.artmarketing.com   <info@artmarketing.com>

Internet 101

A User-Friendly Guide to Exhibiting, Promoting and Selling your Artwork Online

From very beginner to more advanced, this book fills in the gaps about using the worldwide web, e-mail and more.

* Internet lingo
* E-mail communication shortcuts
* Doing business via e-mail
* Creative tricks for research on the web
* Acquiring a URL
* Auctioning on the web
* Designing your site
* Meta tags
* Basic promotional techniques for attracting clients to your site
* Pay-per-click advertising
* Guerrilla tactics
* All about search engines
* Tracking visitors
* Reference sources, including hundreds of sites to browse

Also available in PDF format for $15.95
(no shipping costs)

An extensive section explains tricks of the trade to selling your art on eBay, month after month.

ABOUT THE AUTHORsS
Constance Smith has been working with fine artists for over 21 years, first as an art rep in the San Francisco Bay Area and then as a publisher of books that enable artists to suceed at their chosen career. She has been working on the web for over 10 years now.
Susan Greaves is an artist and has been selling her work on eBay for several years.

$17.95   128-pages   ISBN: 0-940899-97-3   2004 edition $4 shipping

ArtNetwork
530·470·0862   800·383·0677   530·470·0256 Fax
PO Box 1360, Nevada City, CA 95959-1360
www.artmarketing.com   <info@artmarketing.com>

Come see our body of work

Your web page with ArtNetwork will include five reproductions of your artwork (example at right). Each artwork clicks onto an enlarged rendition, approximately three times the size. Two hundred words of copy (whatever you want to say) are allowed.

Our site averages **700 visitors** a day (and going up each quarter), with the gallery being the second most visited area on our site (the first is our main page).

☞ We publicize our site to art publishers, gallery owners, museum curators, consultants, architects, interior designers and more! We receive over **225,000 hits per month.** Your home page on our site will be seen by important members of the art world.

☞ You will have an address that will take your customers directly to your artwork. Your address will have your name in it, i.e., **www.artmarketing.com/gallery/johndoe**

☞ You will want to put this web address on business cards, letterhead, envelopes, brochures, flyers, and any advertising you do. Tell the world where you live on the Internet so they will come see what you do!

To showcase your artwork on-line send:

- **Five images for ArtNetwork to scan; a combination of horizontal and vertical is fine. You can send photo prints/35mm slides/jpgs. Note on slides "top front." If you send a photo/print, it can be no smaller than 2x2", no larger than 8x10". Artwork is electronically scanned and reproduced, using 72 dpi resolution. No color corrections are made, so send well-taken pieces.**
- **A list of the five images: title, size, medium, retail price, and if prints are available, cost and size of prints.**
- **Check, money order or charge card number (VISA/MC/AmExpress/Discover): $220 for two years of service.**
- **Legible copy of no more than 200 words.**
- **E-mail address**
- **A #10 SASE for return of your materials**

ArtNetwork
530·470·0862   800·383·0677   530·470·0256 Fax
PO Box 1360, Nevada City, CA 95959-1360
www.artmarketing.com   <info@artmarketing.com>

www.artmarketing.com

Ivo David
1950 Haines Ave
Union, NJ 07083
908/686-0288 . . . . 908/688-0490 Fax
IVODAVID@aol.com

| The Violet Salesman | NY Central Park II | NY Hot Chestnut Salesman | NY Central Park I | NY Washington Square |

All works copyright of artist.
Click on image or title to enlarge.

Ivo David, painter and poet, and founder of the the new style "Fusionism," received his first art lesson from his father, a well-known artist in Italy. Years later, he accepted an apprenticeship position working with artist Mario Cristini, becaming responsible for set design at the San Carlo Theatre in Naples. He graduated from the Institute of Fine Arts at the Academy of Art in Naples. In 1961 in Caserta, Italy he received a first prize award at the National Art Show for the First Centenary of Unification of Italy by the Ministry of Education. David had his first one-man show at the Galleria del Ponte in Naples. He then moved to the U.S., accepting a teaching position at Seton Hall University. 1963 brought two one-man shows at Seton University gallery; 1963 a one-man show at the Robert Treat Grandroom in Newark, NJ.; 1964 a one-man show at the Crespi Gallery on Madison Ave in NY; 1970 at the Rohrbrach's Mansion in Paris, a one-man show in France at the Salon of Modern Arts in Paris; 1991 Garden State Art Center in New Jersey; 1992 awarded a gold Medal, first prize at the International Juried Show by the Academy of Art Micenei, Italy. David has also been an artistic consultant for various industries and commercial companies. His

Surfing our site

- Visit our site at <u>www.artmarketing.com.</u>

- Visit over 100 artists at <u>www.artmarketing.com/gallery.</u>

- Browse to our book section and find articles to improve your marketing techniques.

- At <u>www.artmarketing.com/Homepg/hotlinks.html</u> you will find leads to residencies, grants, lawyers, consultants, organizations, art fairs, licensing agents, art magazines, museums, galleries, resources and art supplies of all types, info about taxes, special travel adventures for artists and much, much more!

- Sign our guestbook and receive a free article about promoting your site.

ArtNetwork
530·470·0862   800·383·0677   530·470·0256 Fax
PO Box 1360, Nevada City, CA 95959-1360
<u>www.artmarketing.com</u>   <info@artmarketing.com>

Living Artists

In this competitive and fast-paced world, an artist needs to take marketing seriously. Here's a way to do it dynamically and economically! *Living Artists* (formerly titled the *Encyclopedia of Living Artists*) is a direct link to prime customers—including reps, corporate art consultants, gallery owners, interior designers , museum curators and more. These artworld professionals use this book to select artwork throughout the year for various projects. Artwork in the book is reproduced in high-quality full-color, along with artist's name, address and telephone number. Prospective buyers have direct contact with the artist of choice. All fine artists are invited to submit their work. Published biannually in odd-numbered years. A contest is conducted for the cover position. For a prospectus (August 2004 and 2006 deadlines), e-mail your street address to info@artmarketing.com.

ArtNetwork
530·470·0862   800·383·0677   530·470·0256 **Fax**
PO Box 1360, Nevada City, CA 95959-1360
www.artmarketing.com   <info@artmarketing.com>

ArtSource Quarterly

Blast off to success!

Published every three months, this eight-page newsletter is packed full of new ideas (and no advertising) that will give your art business the creative edge, taking your sales to new levels.

Subscribe to *ArtSource Quarterly* for the most current marketing information.

* **Innovative marketing ideas**
* **Hot tips**
* **Interviews with successful artists**
* **Articles by artworld professionals**

Subscription Rates

4 issues (1 year)	$22
8 issues (2 years)	$36
Current issue	$6.50

ArtNetwork
530·470·0862   800·383·0677   530·470·0256 Fax
PO Box 1360, Nevada City, CA 95959-1360
www.artmarketing.com   <info@artmarketing.com>

Art Licensing 101

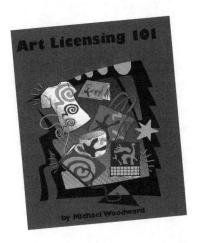

Publishing and Licensing Your Artwork for Profit

Learn how to increase your income by licensing your art. Reaching this industry takes special knowledge. That's exactly what you'll receive in this book: assistance from an expert. The first part of the book has information about conducting business with the publishing and licensing industry; the second part lists contacts in the industry with names, addresses, telephone numbers, web sites and what type of art the company is looking for.

What readers say:

Just wanted you to know that I've bought and read your book and thought it was fabulous! You have so much information in there that it goes beyond helpful. You told me things I didn't even know I didn't know! Thanks so much for making the effort. *Judy*

Art Licensing 101 by Michael Woodward has been the most helpful book since I began this journey. It is a well-written layout of all the important aspects of the licensing industry. The book allows beginners to understand dos and don'ts, legalities, fee structures, importance of copyright and more. I found it especially helpful that he included so many wonderful resources in the book. I highly recommend this book to anyone who is beginning the process of licensing art. *Caroline Simas,* The Creative Palette

You'll learn about:

* **Negotiating fees**
* **How to approach various markets**
* **Targeting your presentation**
* **Trade shows**
* **Licensing agents**
* **Protecting your rights**
* **Self-publishing**

Over 200 listings:

* Calendar publishers
* Licensing agents
* Greeting card publishers
* Print and poster publishers

ABOUT THE AUTHOR

Michael Woodward has worked in the licensing and publishing industry in the U.S. and U.K. for over 25 years. He now lives in Florida and works as a consultant. He also conducts seminars on licensing art.

$23.95   256 pages   ISBN:0-940899-77-2   2003 edition $4 shipping

ArtNetwork
530·470·0862   800·383·0677   530·470·0256 Fax
PO Box 1360, Nevada City, CA 95959-1360
www.artmarketing.com   <info@artmarketing.com>

Art Marketing 101

Learn how to gain exposure as a fine artist. Read about myths many artists fall prey to and how to avoid them. Identify roadblocks to success.
You'll learn about:

* **Preparing a portfolio**
* **Pricing your work**
* **Alternative venues for selling your artwork**
* **Publishing and licensing**
* **Taking care of legal matters**
* **Developing a marketing plan**
* **Publicity matters**
* **Succeeding without a rep**
* **Secrets of successful artists**

Learn what art schools don't teach: **business savvy.** No other book offers artists such concise step-by-step marketing strategies. This book answers such questions as:

* Must I depend on dealers, curators and gallery owners—or can I do it on my own?

* How do I protect my work from plagiarism?

This comprehensive 24-chapter volume covers all the key issues any artist needs to know to do business in today's world and includes:

* Case histories and success stories

* Checklists to help you stay on track

* "Action Plan" at the end of each chapter

What readers say:

How much time, money and heartache could have been saved had I had a copy of Art Marketing 101 years ago. At last the fog has lifted! *Patricia George, Artist, California*

Absolutely everything artists need to know in order to sell their creative work in today's competitive marketplace. Full of excellent tips, practical information and reference material. A must for every artist who wants to make more money. *Sue Viders, Art Marketing Consultant, Colorado*

I highly recommend this book for beginning, emerging and established artists as a reference source for many different topics, as well as for an emotional support. *Synthia Saint James, Artist, California*

ABOUT THE AUTHOR

Constance Smith has been working with fine artists for over 21 years, first as an art rep in the San Francisco Bay Area and then as a publisher of books that enable artists to suceed at their chosen career. She has been working on the web for over 10 years now. All her books are written from a practical viewpoint, enabling artists to begin projects they have put off for years! She periodically lectures around the country.

$24.95   336 pages   ISBN: 0-940899-32-9   2003 edition $4 shipping

ArtNetwork
530·470·0862   800·383·0677   530·470·0256 Fax
PO Box 1360, Nevada City, CA 95959-1360
www.artmarketing.com   <info@artmarketing.com>

www.artmarketing.com